Choc

Cheaper
Than
Therapy

and you don't need
an appointment

Printed in the United States of America
by G&R Publishing Co.

Distributed By:

507 Industrial Street
Waverly, IA 50677

ISBN 1-56383-196-1
Item #7057

Table
of
Contents

Beverages

Iced Cappuccinos

Makes 6 (6-ounce) servings

2/3 C. chocolate syrup
2 C. cold coffee
2 C. vanilla ice cream

Iced cubes or crushed ice
Whipped topping, optional
Cinnamon, optional

In a blender, combine chocolate syrup and cold coffee. Blend at high speed until smooth. Add ice cream and blend until fully incorporated. Fill six glasses 1/3 full with ice cubes or crushed ice. Pour blended mixture over ice in glasses. If desired, garnish with whipped topping and cinnamon.

Iced Mochas

Makes 4 servings

1 1/2 C. cold coffee
2 C. milk
1/4 C. chocolate syrup

1/4 C. sugar
Whipped topping, optional

Pour cold coffee into an ice cube tray and place in freezer until solid. In a blender, combine coffee cubes, milk, chocolate syrup and sugar. Blend until smooth. Pour blended mixture into four glasses. If desired, garnish with whipped topping.

Raspberry Chocolate Smoothies

Makes 4 servings

1 1/2 C. chocolate milk
1 1/2 C. chocolate ice cream
2 1/2 C. frozen unsweetened
    raspberries

1 banana, peeled and sliced
1 to 2 fresh mint leaves,
    chopped

    In a blender, combine chocolate milk, chocolate ice cream, raspberries and sliced banana. Blend until smooth. Pour blended mixture into four glasses. Garnish with chopped mint leaves.

3

Chocolate Polar Bears

Makes 4 servings

2 C. milk
1 C. ice cubes or crushed ice
2/3 C. chocolate syrup

1/2 C. chocolate ice cream
1/4 C. whipped topping,
   divided

In a blender, combine milk, ice cubes, chocolate syrup and chocolate ice cream. Blend until smooth. Pour blended mixture into four glasses. Add 1 tablespoon whipped topping to each glass and stir to swirl blended mixture and whipped topping together.

The 12-step chocoholics program:
Never be more than 12 steps away from chocolate!

Perfectly Chocolate Hot Cocoa

Makes 4 servings

8 tsp. hot cocoa mix, divided
Pinch of salt, divided
8 T. sugar, divided

4 C. milk, divided
1 tsp. vanilla, divided

In each of four coffee mugs, place 2 teaspoons hot cocoa mix, a pinch of salt and 2 tablespoons sugar. Mix well. Pour milk into a large glass measuring cup and heat in microwave for 1 to 1 1/2 minutes, until thoroughly heated. Pour 1 cup hot milk into each mug, stirring constantly. Add 1/4 teaspoon vanilla to each mug and mix well.

Chocolate is nature's way of making up for Mondays.

White Chocolate Hot Cocoa

Makes 4 servings

6 (1 oz.) squares white
    chocolate, chopped
1/4 tsp. cayenne pepper
1/2 tsp. cinnamon

1 egg, beaten
3 1/4 C. milk, divided

In a double boiler over medium heat, place chopped white chocolate. Heat until chocolate is melted and stir in cayenne pepper and cinnamon. Add beaten egg and whisk until smooth. Gradually add 1 cup milk and heat, whisking constantly, for 2 minutes. Gradually add remaining 2 1/4 cups milk and stir until heated throughout. Make sure not to let mixture simmer or boil to avoid a skin from forming on top of milk. Pour hot mixture into four coffee mugs. If desired, garnish with additional cinnamon on top.

Chemically speaking, chocolate really is the world's perfect food.

French Vanilla Mochas

Makes 4 servings

3 C. water
1/4 C. instant coffee granules
1 C. French vanilla liquid
    creamer

1/4 C. chocolate syrup
Whipped topping, optional

In a medium saucepan over medium heat, heat water. Add instant coffee and mix well, stirring until instant coffee is dissolved. Add French vanilla liquid creamer and chocolate syrup and mix well. Pour hot mixture into four coffee mugs. If desired, garnish with whipped topping.

Hot Cocoa Mochas

Makes 2 servings

1/4 C. sugar
2 T. hot cocoa mix
2 T. water

1 C. whipped topping
2 C. hot brewed coffee

In a large glass measuring cup, combine sugar and hot cocoa mix. Add water and stir until well blended. Microwave on high for 30 to 45 seconds, until thoroughly heated. Add whipped topping and stir until blended. Return to microwave for an additional minute, until heated throughout. Pour 1 cup hot brewed coffee into each of two coffee mugs. Divide hot mixture into mugs and mix well.

A man found a bottle on the beach, opened it and out popped a genie who gave him three wishes. The man wished for a million dollars, and poof!, there was a million dollars. He wished for a convertible, and poof!, there was a convertible. And third, he wished he could be irresistible to all women, and poof!, ... he turned into a box of chocolates.

Chocolate Caramel Cappuccinos

Makes 4 servings

2 C. water
1 1/2 C. milk
1/4 C. chocolate syrup

6 T. caramel topping
2 T. instant coffee granules

In a large glass measuring cup or bowl, place water, milk, chocolate syrup, caramel topping and instant coffee granules. Microwave on high for 2 to 3 minutes, stirring after every minute, until thoroughly heated. Remove mixture from microwave and mix well. Pour hot mixture into four coffee mugs.

Strength is the capacity to break a chocolate bar into four pieces with your bare hands... and then eat just one of the pieces.

Spicy Hot Chocolate

Makes 4 servings

4 (1 oz.) env. instant hot
    chocolate mix
4 tsp. vanilla, divided
4 tsp. nutmeg, divided
6 tsp. cinnamon, divided

1/4 C. brown sugar, divided
1/4 C. sweetened condensed
    milk, divided
4 C. hot water, divided

In each of four coffee mugs, place 1 envelope instant hot chocolate mix, 1 teaspoon vanilla, 1 teaspoon nutmeg, 1 1/2 teaspoons cinnamon, 1 tablespoon brown sugar and 1 tablespoon sweetened condensed milk. Mix well. Pour 1 cup hot water into each mug, stirring constantly.

Chocolate Peanut Butter Milkshakes

Makes 4 servings

1 C. creamy peanut butter
1/4 C. chocolate syrup

1/4 C. milk
12 ice cubes

In a blender, combine peanut butter, chocolate syrup, milk and ice cubes. Blend until smooth. Pour blended mixture into four glasses.

Chocolate Mint Milkshakes

Makes 4 servings

8 scoops vanilla ice cream
1/2 C. milk

1/2 C. chocolate syrup
4 drops peppermint extract

In a blender, combine vanilla ice cream, milk, chocolate syrup and peppermint extract. Blend until smooth. Pour blended mixture into four glasses.

Strawberry Banana Chocolate Milkshakes

Makes 4 servings

2 C. milk
1 C. frozen unsweetened
    strawberries
1 ripe banana, peeled
    and sliced

1/4 C. powdered chocolate
    drink mix
1 tsp. vanilla
4 tsp. sugar

In a blender, combine milk, strawberries, sliced banana, chocolate drink mix, vanilla and sugar. Blend until smooth. If mixture is too runny, additional strawberries may be added. Pour blended mixture into four glasses.

I'll eat anything, as long as it's chocolate.

Chocolate Buzz Milkshakes

Makes 4 servings

2 C. milk
10 ice cubes
2 oz. brewed espresso

1 1/2 C. chocolate ice cream
4 tsp. instant hot chocolate mix
1/4 C. chocolate syrup

In a blender, combine milk, ice cubes and espresso. Blend until smooth and add chocolate ice cream, instant hot chocolate mix and chocolate syrup. Blend until fully incorporated. Pour blended mixture into four glasses.

Chocolate Cake Shooter

Makes 1 shot

1 oz. hazelnut liqueur
1/2 oz. vodka

1 lemon wedge
Sugar

Into a shot glass, pour hazelnut liqueur and vodka. Coat lemon wedge with sugar. To drink, suck on sugar coated lemon wedge and shoot the drink. Should taste just like chocolate cake in your mouth!

B-52 Shooter

Makes 2 shots

1 (1 1/2 oz.) jigger Irish
cream liqueur

1 (1 1/2 oz.) jigger dark
Crème de Cacao

In a cocktail shaker or glass, combine Irish cream liqueur and Crème de Cacao. Shake or stir and pour evenly into 2 shot glasses. If desired, may substitute 1 1/2 ounces Kahlua for jigger of Crème de Cacao.

Nuts take up space where chocolate ought to be.

Mint Chocolate Shooter

Makes 1 shot

3/4 oz. Irish cream liqueur　　**1/4 oz. Crème de Menthe**
1/2 oz. white Crème de Cacao

Into a shot glass, pour Irish crème liqueur. Add white Crème de Cacao and Crème de Menthe liqueur.

Chocolate Martini

Makes 2 servings

4 oz. dark Crème de　　**1 (1 oz.) square semi-sweet**
**　　Cacao or Kahlua**　　**　　chocolate, grated**
3 oz. vodka　　**Chocolate syrup, optional**
Ice

In a cocktail shaker, combine Crème de Cacao and vodka. Add ice and shake vigorously. Strain mixture into 2 chilled martini glasses. Garnish with grated chocolate. If desired, drizzle a little chocolate syrup over martinis.

Mudslides

Makes 4 servings

4 C. vanilla ice cream   **1 1/2 C. Kahlua**
1 1/2 C. Irish cream liqueur   **1/3 C. chocolate syrup**

In a large mixing bowl, combine vanilla ice cream, Irish cream liqueur, Kahlua and chocolate syrup at low speed. Mix slowly, leaving some ice cream lumps. Cover the bottom of four glasses with additional chocolate syrup. Pour blended mixture into glasses.

Indiana Bulldogs

Makes 2 servings

2 oz. vodka, divided   **2/3 C. milk, divided**
2 oz. dark Crème de   **2/3 C. cola, divided**
  Cacao or Kahlua, divided

Fill each of two tall glasses half full with ice. Add 1 ounce vodka, 1 ounce Crème de Cacao, 1/3 cup milk and 1/3 cup cola to each glass. Mix well.

Calypso Coffee

Makes 2 servings

2 oz. rum
2 oz. dark Crème de Cacao

2 C. hot brewed coffee

In a small saucepan, combine rum, Crème de Cacao and hot coffee. Mix well and pour mixture into two coffee mugs.

Moscow Hot Chocolate

Makes 4 servings

4 oz. vanilla flavored
vodka, divided
3 oz. Amaretto liqueur,
divided

1/4 C. instant hot chocolate
mix, divided
3 C. milk, divided

In each of four coffee mugs, place 1 ounce vodka, 3/4 ounce Amaretto liqueur and 1 tablespoon instant hot chocolate mix. Mix well. Pour milk into a large glass measuring cup and heat in microwave for 1 to 1 1/2 minutes, until thoroughly heated. Pour 3/4 cup hot milk into each mug, stirring constantly.

Chocolate Coffee Kiss

Makes 2 servings

1 1/2 oz. Kahlua
1 1/2 oz. Irish cream liqueur
1 oz. dark Crème de Cacao
2 tsp. Grand Marnier
2 C. hot brewed coffee,
    divided

1/4 C. whipped topping,
    divided
2 T. chocolate syrup, divided
2 maraschino cherries,
    divided

Into a cocktail shaker, pour Kahlua, Irish cream liqueur, Crème de Cacao and Grand Marnier. Shake vigorously and pour evenly into two coffee mugs. Pour 1 cup hot brewed coffee into each mug and mix well. Top each serving with 2 tablespoons whipped topping, 1 tablespoon chocolate syrup and 1 maraschino cherry.

If life is like a box of chocolate, then it's time for me to buy another box... I seem to have already devoured all the good ones.

Breads
& Muffins

Chocolate Round Bread

Makes 2 loaves

1 T. sunflower seed oil	6 C. bread flour
2 tsp. salt	4 1/2 T. sugar
1 3/4 C. warm water (110°F)	3/4 C. cocoa powder
1 (1/4 oz.) pkg. instant yeast	

Preheat oven to 425°. In a large bowl, combine sunflower seed oil, salt, warm water, instant yeast, bread flour, sugar and cocoa powder. Mix well with a wooden spoon until a soft dough forms. Turn out dough onto a flat floured surface. Knead dough for 5 minutes, until smooth and elastic. Divide dough into two parts and roll each half into a ball. Place each ball on a greased baking sheet. Cut a criss-cross pattern in the tops of each ball and cover with a towel. Let dough rise until doubled in size. Bake in oven for 35 minutes. Let cool slightly before removing to wire racks.

There's nothing better than a good friend...except a good friend with chocolate!

Bread Machine Chocolate Chip Bread

Makes 1 loaf

1/4 C. warm water
1 C. milk
1 egg
2 T. margarine, softened
3 C. bread flour
3 T. brown sugar

2 T. sugar
1 tsp. salt
1 tsp. cinnamon
1 1/2 tsp. active dry yeast
3/4 C. chocolate chips

In the pan of bread machine, place warm water, milk, egg and margarine. Add bread flour, brown sugar, sugar, salt and cinnamon. Make a well in the center of the dry ingredients and add yeast. Do not mix. Select the setting that allows ingredients to be folded into the dough and press Start. Add chocolate chips at the signal, or about 5 minutes before the kneading cycle has completed. Close bread machine and let bake.

Banana Chocolate Bread

Makes 2 loaves

1 C. margarine, softened
2 C. sugar
4 eggs
6 bananas, peeled and
    mashed
2 tsp. vanilla

3 C. flour
2 tsp. baking soda
1/4 C. cocoa powder
1 C. sour cream
1 C. chocolate chips

Preheat oven to 350°. Lightly grease two 5x9" loaf pans and set aside. In a large bowl, cream together margarine, sugar and eggs. Add mashed bananas and vanilla. Sift in flour, baking soda and cocoa powder. Mix well and add sour cream and chocolate chips. Pour batter evenly into prepared pans. Bake in oven for 60 minutes, or until a toothpick inserted in center of loaves comes out clean. Let cool slightly before removing to wire racks.

*Life without chocolate is like
a beach without water.*

Cherry Cranberry Chocolate Chip Bread

Makes 3 miniature loaves

1 C. chocolate chips
1 C. fresh or frozen
    cranberries,
    coarsely chopped
1/2 C. chopped pecans
2 tsp. grated orange peel
2 C. flour
1 C. sugar

1 1/2 tsp. baking powder
1/2 tsp. baking soda
1/2 tsp. salt
2 T. shortening, softened
3/4 C. orange juice
1 egg, lightly beaten
Cocoa Drizzle Glaze,
    optional

Preheat oven to 350°. Lightly grease and flour three 3x5" miniature loaf pans. In a small bowl, combine chocolate chips, cranberries, chopped pecans and grated orange peel and set aside. In a large bowl, combine flour, sugar, baking powder, baking soda and salt. Using a pastry blender, cut in shortening until mixture resembles coarse crumbs. Stir in orange juice, egg and chocolate chips mixture. Mix until fully incorporated. Pour batter evenly into prepared pans. Bake in oven for 40 to 45 minutes, or until a toothpick inserted in center of loaves comes out clean. Let cool for 15 minutes before removing to a wire rack. If desired, top with Cocoa Drizzle Glaze.

Cocoa Drizzle Glaze

1 T. butter or margarine
1 T. cocoa powder
1 T. water

1/2 C. powdered sugar
1/2 tsp. vanilla

In a small microwave safe bowl, place butter. Microwave for 20 to 30 seconds, until butter is melted. Stir in cocoa powder and water. Microwave for an additional 15 to 30 seconds, until mixture is slightly thickened. Gradually add powdered sugar and vanilla, stirring constantly, until glaze is smooth. If glaze is too thick, add a few drops of water. Drizzle over Cherry Cranberry Chocolate Chip Bread.

Banana Nut Chocolate Chip Bread

Makes 1 loaf

1 1/2 C. flour
1 C. sugar
1/8 C. cocoa powder
1 tsp. baking soda
1 tsp. cinnamon
1/2 C. finely chopped pecans
1/2 C. chocolate chips

2 eggs
1/2 C. butter, melted
3 medium bananas, mashed
1/2 C. plain yogurt or sour
   cream
1 tsp. vanilla

Preheat oven to 350°. Lightly grease and flour a 5x9" loaf pan and set aside. In a medium bowl, combine flour, sugar, cocoa powder, baking soda, cinnamon, chopped pecans and chocolate chips. In a large bowl, beat eggs at low speed until fluffy. Add melted butter, mashed bananas, yogurt and vanilla. Add dry ingredients to banana mixture, blending until moistened. Pour batter into prepared pan. Bake in oven for 45 to 50 minutes, or until a toothpick inserted in center of loaf comes out clean. Let cool in pan before removing to a wire rack.

There are four basic food groups: milk chocolate, dark chocolate, white chocolate and chocolate truffles!

Chocolate Zucchini Bread

Makes 2 loaves

2 (1 oz.) squares unsweetened
    chocolate, melted
3 C. flour
1 tsp. salt
1 tsp. cinnamon
1/4 tsp. baking powder
1 tsp. baking soda

3 eggs
2 C. sugar
1 C. vegetable oil
1 tsp. vanilla
2 C. grated zucchini
1 C. chopped almonds

Preheat oven to 350°. Grease two 5x9" loaf pans and set aside. In a double boiler over medium heat, melt chocolate squares and set aside to cool. Into a medium bowl, sift flour, salt, cinnamon, baking powder and baking soda. In a large bowl, beat eggs until lemon colored and add sugar and oil. Mix well and add vanilla, grated zucchini and cooled chocolate. Stir in flour mixture and add chopped almonds. Mix well and pour batter into prepared pans. Bake in oven for 60 minutes, or until a toothpick inserted in center of loaves comes out clean. Let cool in pans for 15 minutes before removing to a wire rack.

Pumpkin Chocolate Chip Bread

Makes 3 loaves

3 C. sugar
1 (15 oz.) can pumpkin puree
1 C. vegetable oil
2/3 C. water
4 eggs
3 1/2 C. flour
1 T. cinnamon

1 T. nutmeg
2 tsp. baking soda
1 1/2 tsp. salt
1 C. miniature chocolate
  chips
1/2 C. chopped walnuts,
  optional

Preheat oven to 350°. Grease and flour three 5x9" loaf pans. In a large bowl, combine sugar, pumpkin puree, vegetable oil, water and eggs. Beat until smooth and add flour, cinnamon, nutmeg, baking soda and salt. Mix well and gently fold in chocolate chips and chopped walnuts. Pour mixture into prepared pans. Bake in oven for 1 hour, or until a toothpick inserted in center of loaves comes out clean. Let cool in pans before removing to wire racks.

Stress wouldn't be so hard to take if it were covered in chocolate.

Apple Chocolate Bread

Makes 1 loaf

1 C. plus 2 T. sugar, divided
3/4 tsp. cinnamon, divided
3/4 C. chopped walnuts,
    divided
2 C. flour
1/2 tsp. salt
1/2 tsp. baking powder
1/2 tsp. baking soda

1/4 tsp. nutmeg
1/2 C. butter or margarine,
    softened
2 eggs
1 tsp. vanilla
2 T. buttermilk
1 C. chopped apples
1/4 C. chocolate chips

Preheat oven to 350°. To make topping, in a small bowl, combine 2 tablespoons sugar, 1/4 teaspoon cinnamon and 1/4 cup chopped walnuts. Mix well and set aside. In a medium bowl, combine flour, salt, baking powder, baking soda, remaining 1/2 teaspoon cinnamon and nutmeg. In a large bowl, cream together butter and remaining 1 cup sugar. Add eggs and vanilla and mix well. Alternating, add flour mixture and buttermilk to butter mixture, stirring constantly. Stir in chopped apples, remaining 1/2 cup chopped walnuts and chocolate chips. Pour into a greased 5x9" loaf pan. Sprinkle topping mixture over batter. Bake in oven for 50 to 60 minutes, or until a toothpick inserted in center of loaf comes out clean. Let cool in pan before removing to a wire rack.

Fruit Fields Cocoa Glaze Bread

Makes 2 loaves

1/2 C. butter or margarine, softened
1 C. sugar
2 eggs
1 tsp. vanilla
2 C. flour
1 tsp. baking soda
1/4 tsp. salt

3 medium bananas, mashed
1/2 C. chopped maraschino cherries, drained
1 (11 oz.) can mandarin orange sections, drained
1/2 C. chopped figs or dates
1 C. chocolate chips
Cocoa Glaze, optional

Preheat oven to 350°. Lightly grease two 4x8" loaf pans and set aside. In a large bowl, cream together butter and sugar. Add eggs and vanilla and mix well. In a medium bowl, combine flour, baking soda and salt. Alternating, add flour mixture and mashed bananas, stirring constantly. Stir in chopped cherries, mandarin oranges, chopped figs and chocolate chips. Pour batter evenly into prepared pans. Bake in oven for 40 to 50 minutes, or until loaves are golden brown. Let cool in pans before removing to wire racks. If desired, top with Cocoa Glaze.

Cocoa Glaze

2 T. butter or margarine
2 T. light corn syrup
3 T. water

3 T. cocoa powder
2 tsp. vanilla
1 1/2 C. powdered sugar

In a small saucepan over low heat, melt butter and stir in corn syrup. Add water and cocoa powder and mix well. Cook until thickened. Remove from heat and stir in vanilla. Gradually add powdered sugar until glaze reaches desired consistency. Drizzle over Fruit Fields Cocoa Glaze Bread.

Mocha Chip Loaf

Makes 1 loaf

1 T. hot water
2 tsp. French vanilla instant
    coffee granules
2 1/4 C. flour
1 1/2 tsp. baking powder
1/2 tsp. salt

3/4 C. miniature
    chocolate chips
3/4 C. sugar
1/2 C. butter, softened
2 eggs
1 C. buttermilk

Preheat oven to 350°. In a small bowl, combine hot water and instant coffee granules, mixing until granules are dissolved. In a medium bowl, combine flour, baking powder, salt and chocolate chips and set aside. In a large mixing bowl, beat sugar and butter at medium speed until creamy. Add coffee mixture and eggs, mixing well. Reduce speed to low and gradually add flour mixture, alternating with buttermilk. Pour batter into prepared pan. Bake in oven for 55 to 60 minutes, or until a toothpick inserted in center of loaf comes out clean. Let cool in pan before removing to a wire rack.

Chocolate Date Loaf

Makes 1 loaf

1 C. pitted and chopped dates
3/4 C. boiling water
1 tsp. baking soda
1 3/4 C. flour
1 tsp. baking powder
1/2 C. chopped walnuts
1 egg

3/4 tsp. salt
1/2 C. sugar
1 tsp. vanilla
3/4 C. chocolate chips,
    melted
1/4 C. butter, melted

Preheat oven to 350°. Lightly grease a 5x9" loaf pan and set aside. In a medium bowl, combine chopped dates, boiling water and baking soda. Set aside to cool. In a separate bowl, whisk together flour, baking powder and chopped walnuts. In a large mixing bowl, beat together egg, salt, sugar and vanilla at low speed. Add melted chocolate chips and melted butter and mix well. Stir in cooled dates mixture and flour mixture and mix until well combined. Pour batter into prepared pan. Bake in oven for 1 hour, or until a toothpick inserted in center of loaf comes out clean. Let cool in pan before removing to a wire rack.

Chocolate Muffins

Makes 14 muffins

1 1/2 C. flour
3/4 C. sugar
1/4 C. cocoa powder
2 tsp. baking powder
1 tsp. baking soda

1/2 tsp. salt
2/3 C. vanilla yogurt
2/3 C. milk
1/2 tsp. vanilla
Powdered sugar, optional

Preheat oven to 400°. Line 2 1/2" muffin cups with paper liners. In a medium bowl, combine flour, sugar, cocoa powder, baking powder, baking soda and salt. Mix well and stir in yogurt, milk and vanilla. Mix until just combined. Pour batter into prepared muffin cups. Bake in oven for 15 to 20 minutes, or until a toothpick inserted in center of muffins comes out clean. Let cool slightly in pans before removing to wire racks. If desired, sift powdered sugar over tops of muffins.

It's not that chocolates are a substitute for love. Love is a substitute for chocolate. Chocolate is, let's face it, more reliable that a man.

Chocolate Filled Muffins

Makes 1 dozen

2 C. flour
3/4 C. sugar
1/4 C. cocoa powder
3 tsp. baking powder
1/2 tsp. salt
1/2 tsp. cinnamon
1 egg

1 C. milk
1/3 C. vegetable oil
1/4 C. instant powdered milk
2 T. hot water
1 tsp. butter
1/4 tsp. almond extract
1 C. shredded coconut

Preheat oven to 400°. Lightly grease twelve muffin cups. In a large bowl, combine flour, sugar, cocoa powder, baking powder, salt and cinnamon. In a small bowl, lightly beat egg and add milk and vegetable oil. Make a well in the center of the flour mixture and add egg mixture to well, stirring until batter is moistened. Pour batter into prepared muffin cups. In a small bowl, combine powdered milk and hot water. Mix vigorously to blend well. Add butter and almond extract. Stir in shredded coconut. Form mixture into twelve balls. Push one ball into the batter in each muffin cup. Bake in oven for 20 to 25 minutes. Let cool slightly before removing to wire racks.

Chocolate doesn't make the world go round...but it certainly makes the ride worthwhile!

Fudgey Peanut Butter Chip Muffins

Makes about 15 muffins

1/2 C. applesauce
1/2 C. quick cooking oats
1/4 C. butter or margarine,
   softened
1/2 C. sugar
1/2 C. brown sugar
1 egg

1/2 tsp. vanilla
3/4 C. flour
1/4 C. cocoa powder
1/2 tsp. baking soda
1/4 tsp. cinnamon, optional
1 C. peanut butter chips
Powdered sugar, optional

Preheat oven to 350°. Line 2 1/2" muffin cups with paper liners. In a small bowl, combine applesauce and oats and set aside. In a large bowl, cream together butter, sugar, brown sugar, egg and vanilla, mixing until well blended. Add applesauce mixture and stir until well combined. Stir in flour, cocoa powder, baking soda and cinnamon. Fold in peanut butter chips. Pour batter into prepared muffin cups. Bake in oven for 22 to 26 minutes, or until a toothpick inserted in center of muffins comes out clean. Let cool slightly in pans before removing to wire racks. If desired, sift powdered sugar over tops of muffins.

Chocolate Streusel Pecan Muffins

Makes 1 dozen

1 1/4 C. flour, divided
1/4 C. brown sugar
1/2 tsp. cinnamon, divided
5 T. butter, melted, divided
1 C. chopped pecans, divided
1 (11 1/2 oz.) pkg. milk
    chocolate chips, divided

1/3 C. milk
2 T. sugar
2 tsp. baking powder
1 egg
1/2 tsp. vanilla

Preheat oven to 375°. Line twelve muffins cups with paper liners and set aside. In a small bowl, combine 1/4 cup flour, brown sugar, 1/4 teaspoon cinnamon and 2 tablespoons melted butter. Stir until mixture resembles coarse crumbs. Stir in 1/4 cup chopped pecans and set aside. In a double boiler over medium heat, combine 1 cup chocolate chips, milk and remaining 3 tablespoons butter. Stir until chocolate is melted and mixture is smooth. In a large bowl, combine remaining 1 cup flour, sugar, baking powder, remaining 1/4 teaspoon cinnamon, remaining 3/4 cup chopped pecans and remaining chocolate chips. In a small bowl, combine egg, vanilla and melted chocolate mixture. Add egg mixture to ingredients in large bowl. Mix well and pour into prepared muffin cups. Sprinkle topping mixture over batter. Bake in oven for 20 to 25 minutes, or until a toothpick inserted in center of muffins comes out clean. Let cool slightly in pans before removing to wire racks.

Oatmeal Chocolate Chip Muffins

Makes 1 dozen

1 1/4 C. quick cooking oats
1 1/4 C. milk
1 egg
1/2 C. vegetable oil
3/4 C. brown sugar, divided

3/4 C. chocolate chips
1 C. chopped pecans, divided
1 1/4 C. flour
4 tsp. baking powder
1 tsp. salt

Preheat oven to 400°. Grease twelve muffin cups and set aside. In a medium bowl, combine oats and milk. Set aside for 15 minutes. In a separate bowl, combine egg, vegetable oil, 1/2 cup brown sugar, chocolate chips and 1/2 cup chopped pecans. After 15 minutes, add milk and oats mixture to egg mixture. In a medium bowl, combine flour, baking powder and salt. Add flour mixture to oats mixture and stir just until moistened. Pour batter into prepared muffin cups. Sprinkle remaining 1/4 cup brown sugar and remaining 1/2 cup chopped pecans over batter. Bake in oven for 20 to 25 minutes. Let cool slightly in pans before removing to wire racks.

Mocha Chocolate Chip Banana Muffins

Makes 1 1/2 dozen

1 T. instant coffee granules
1 T. hot water
1 C. butter or margarine,
 softened
1 1/4 C. sugar
1 egg
3 ripe bananas, peeled

1 tsp. vanilla
2 1/4 C. flour
1/4 tsp. salt
1 tsp. baking powder
1 tsp. baking soda
1 C. chocolate chips

Preheat oven to 350°. Grease fifteen to eighteen muffin cups and set aside. In a small bowl, combine instant coffee granules and hot water, mixing until coffee is dissolved. In a blender or food processor, combine butter, sugar, egg, bananas, vanilla and coffee mixture. Blend for 2 minutes. Add flour, salt, baking powder and baking soda. Blend just until flour disappears. Stir in chocolate chips with a wooden spoon. Spoon mixture into prepared muffin cups. Bake in oven for 25 minutes. Let cool slightly in pans before removing to wire racks.

Chocolate: a luscious, lumpy, load of love.

Chocolate Chip Biscuits with Berries N' Bananas

Makes 8 servings

2 C. flour
1/2 C. plus 2 T. sugar,
   divided
1 T. baking powder
1/2 tsp. salt
1/2 C. cold butter
1/4 C. vegetable shortening

2/3 C. heavy whipping cream
1/2 C. miniature chocolate
   chips
1 pint strawberries, hulled
   and sliced
1 1/2 C. whipped topping
2 bananas, peeled and sliced

Preheat oven to 400°. In a large bowl, combine flour, 1/2 cup sugar, baking powder and salt. Using a pastry blender, cut in butter and vegetable shortening until mixture resembles coarse crumbs. Stir in heavy whipping cream, mixing just until moistened. Stir in chocolate chips. Turn dough out on a lightly floured flat surface. Knead dough for 1 minute, until smooth. Roll dough out to 3/4" thickness and, using a 2 1/2" biscuit cutter, cut into 8 biscuits. Place biscuits 1" apart on an ungreased baking sheet. Bake in oven for 10 to 14 minutes, until lightly browned. Remove from oven and let cool slightly. In a medium bowl, toss sliced strawberries with remaining 2 tablespoons sugar. To serve, split biscuits in half. Spoon whipped topping onto bottom half of each biscuit. Top with strawberries and banana slices and set top half of biscuit over fruit.

Hazelnut Chocolate Chip Scones

Makes 8 scones

2 C. flour
1/3 C. brown sugar
1 1/2 tsp. baking powder
1/2 tsp. baking soda
1/4 tsp. salt
6 T. cold butter,
    cut into pieces

1/2 C. buttermilk
1 egg
1 1/2 tsp. almond extract
1 C. chocolate chips
1/2 C. chopped hazelnuts

Preheat oven to 400°. Lightly grease a 9" diameter circle in the center of a baking sheet and set aside. In a large bowl, combine flour, brown sugar, baking powder, baking soda and salt. Using a pastry blender, cut in butter pieces. In a separate bowl, combine buttermilk, egg and almond extract. Add to flour mixture and stir until combined. Fold in chocolate chips and chopped hazelnuts. The dough should be sticky. Spread dough into an 8" diameter circle on prepared baking sheet. Using a serrated knife, cut into 8 wedges. Bake for 17 to 19 minutes, or until tops of scones are lightly browned. Let cool on baking sheet before removing to a wire rack. If necessary, re-cut circle into 8 scones.

Double Chocolate Cake Scones

Makes 8 scones

3 C. flour
1/4 C. sugar
4 tsp. baking powder
1/4 tsp. salt
1/2 C. butter or margarine,
   cut into pieces

3 eggs
1/2 C. milk
3/4 C. miniature chocolate
   chips, divided
1 T. grated orange peel
1/4 C. white chocolate chips

Preheat oven to 450°. Grease a large baking sheet and set aside. In a large bowl, combine flour, sugar, baking powder and salt. Using a pastry blender, cut in butter pieces. In a separate bowl, combine eggs and milk and add to flour mixture. Fold in 1/2 cup chocolate chips and grated orange peel. Spread dough into an 8" diameter circle on prepared baking sheet. Using a serrated knife, cut into 8 wedges. Bake for 20 to 25 minutes, or until tops of scones are lightly browned. Let cool on baking sheet before removing to a wire rack. If necessary, re-cut circle into 8 scones. In a double boiler over medium heat, combine remaining 1/4 cup chocolate chips and white chocolate chips, stirring until melted. Drizzle melted chocolate over scones.

Nine out of ten people like chocolate.
The tenth person always lies.

Chocolate Turnovers

Makes 1 1/2 dozen

2 C. chocolate chips, divided
1 tsp. cinnamon
1 (17 oz.) pkg. frozen
    puff pastry, thawed

1 egg
2 tsp. water
1 1/2 tsp. vegetable
    shortening

Preheat oven to 400°. In a small bowl, combine 1 1/2 cups chocolate chips and cinnamon and set aside. Unfold one puff pastry sheet and roll out to a 12" square. Cut square into nine 4" squares. Place 1 heaping tablespoonful of the chocolate chip mixture onto the center of each square. In a small bowl, beat egg with a fork and mix with water. Lightly brush the edges of each square with the egg mixture. Fold squares over diagonally and seal the edges. Repeat with remaining puff pastry square and chocolate chip mixture, making eighteen turnovers. Lightly brush tops of turnovers with egg mixture and place turnovers on ungreased baking sheets. Bake in oven for 15 minutes or until light golden brown. Remove to a wire rack to cool. In a double boiler over medium heat, combine remaining 1/2 cup chocolate chips and vegetable shortening. Heat, stirring frequently, until completely melted. Drizzle melted chocolate mixture over turnovers.

A little too much chocolate
is just about right.

Cookies

No-Bake Chocolate Oatmeal Drops

Makes 4 dozen

1/2 C. butter
1/2 C. milk
2 C. sugar
1/2 C. peanut butter
3 C. quick cooking oats

5 T. cocoa powder
1/2 C. chopped walnuts,
**   raisins or shredded**
**   coconut, optional**

In a large saucepan over medium heat, combine butter, milk and sugar. Bring to a boil for 1 1/2 minutes. Remove from heat and stir in peanut butter, oats and cocoa powder. If desired, stir in chopped walnuts, raisins or shredded coconut. Mix well. Drop mixture by tablespoonfuls onto waxed paper. Cookies will harden as they cool.

What use are cartridges in battle? I always carry chocolate instead. ~ George Bernard Shaw

Peanut Chocolate Cookies

Makes 3 dozen

1/2 C. butter
1/2 C. peanut butter
1/2 tsp. vanilla
1 C. brown sugar
1 egg
3/4 C. flour

1/3 C. cocoa powder
1 tsp. baking soda
6 (1 oz.) squares milk
 chocolate, coarsely
 chopped
1 1/2 C. salted peanuts

Preheat oven to 350°. Lightly grease baking sheets and set aside. In a large bowl, cream together butter, peanut butter and vanilla. Mix in brown sugar and egg, stirring until well combined. In a separate bowl, combine flour, cocoa powder and baking soda and add to peanut butter mixture. Fold in chopped chocolate and peanuts. Mix well. Lightly wet hands under cold water. Roll teaspoonfuls of dough into balls. Place balls 2" apart on prepared baking sheets. Flatten balls slightly and bake in oven for 12 minutes. Transfer cookies to wire racks to cool.

*Among life's mysteries is how
a two pound box of chocolate can
make a woman gain five pounds.*

Mint Chocolate Crunches

Makes 4 dozen

48 small chocolate-covered
    peppermint patties
1 C. chocolate chips
2 C. flour
2/3 C. butter, softened
1/4 C. light corn syrup

2 tsp. baking soda
1/4 tsp. salt
1 egg
1/2 C. plus 1/3 C. sugar,
    divided

Unwrap chocolate-covered peppermint patties and set aside. In a small heavy saucepan over low heat, place chocolate chips, stirring frequently, until melted and smooth. Transfer melted chocolate to a large mixing bowl and add flour, butter, corn syrup, baking soda, salt, egg and 1/2 cup sugar. Beat at low speed until blended. Increase speed to medium and beat until well mixed. Gather dough into a ball and wrap in plastic wrap. Place in refrigerator for 2 hours. Preheat oven to 350°. In a small bowl, place remaining 1/3 cup sugar. Shape dough into 96 balls. Roll each ball in sugar to coat. Place balls 2" apart on ungreased baking sheets. Bake in oven for 12 to 15 minutes or until set. Immediately remove half of the cookies from baking sheets and invert on a flat surface. While still hot, place one peppermint patty on each cookie and top with another cookie. Press cookies together slightly so mint patty spreads out and melts. Set cookies on wire racks to cool.

Hollow chocolate has no calories.

Chocolate Toffee Cookies

Makes 2 dozen

1 (18 1/4 oz.) pkg. devil's
food cake mix
1/3 C. vegetable oil
2 eggs

3/4 C. coarsely chopped
chocolate-covered
toffee candy bars

Preheat oven to 350°. Lightly grease baking sheets and set aside. In a large mixing bowl, combine devil's food cake mix, vegetable oil and eggs. Beat at low speed for 3 to 4 minutes, until well blended. Using a wooden spoon, stir in chopped candy bars. Drop dough by teaspoonfuls 2" apart onto prepared baking sheets. Bake in oven for 9 to 11 minutes, until cookies are firm. Set cookies on wire racks to cool.

Frosted Chocolate Walnut Cookies

Makes 4 dozen

1 (5 oz.) pkg. non-instant
  chocolate pudding mix
3 C. Bisquick baking mix
3/4 C. sugar
6 T. butter, softened

2 eggs
1/2 C. milk
1 1/2 tsp. vanilla
2 C. shredded coconut
Chocolate Frosting, optional

Preheat oven to 350°. Lightly grease baking sheets and set aside. In a large bowl, combine chocolate pudding mix, baking mix and sugar. In a medium saucepan over medium heat, place butter. Heat until butter is melted and remove from heat. Stir in eggs, milk and vanilla. Add butter mixture to pudding mixture. Add shredded coconut and mix well. Drop dough by rounded teaspoonfuls onto prepared baking sheets. Bake in oven for 12 to 14 minutes. Set cookies on wire racks to cool. If desired, frost cookies with Chocolate Frosting.

Chocolate Frosting

5 1/3 T. butter, softened
1/2 C. cocoa powder
Pinch of salt

3 T. boiling water
1 1/2 C. powdered sugar

In a large bowl, cream the butter. Add cocoa powder, salt and boiling water, stirring until smooth. Stir in powdered sugar until frosting reaches desired consistency. If frosting is too thick, add a little water. If frosting is too thin, add a little more powdered sugar. Spread over Frosted Chocolate Walnut Cookies.

Nutty Chocolate Chip Goodies

Makes 4 dozen

1 C. butter, softened
1 C. brown sugar
1 C. sugar
2 eggs
2 T. milk
2 tsp. vanilla
2 C. flour

1 tsp. baking powder
1 tsp. baking soda
1 tsp. salt
2 C. quick cooking oats
2 C. chocolate chips
1 C. coarsely chopped
    walnuts

In a large bowl, cream together butter, brown sugar and sugar, mixing until lightened. Stir in eggs, milk and vanilla and mix until well combined. Into a separate bowl, sift flour, baking powder, baking soda and salt. Add dry ingredients to creamed mixture, stirring just until blended. Add oats and mix well. Fold in chocolate chips and chopped walnuts. Cover dough and refrigerate for at least 1 hour. Preheat oven to 350°. Grease baking sheets. Shape dough into balls and place 2" apart on prepared baking sheets. Bake in oven until lightly browned, about 10 minutes. Let cookies cool slightly on baking sheets before removing to wire racks.

In the cookies of life, friends are the chocolate chips.

Waffle Iron Chocolate Cookies

Makes 2 dozen

2 (1 oz.) squares unsweetened chocolate	1/2 C. flour 1 tsp. baking powder
1 C. brown sugar	1/2 tsp. salt
1/2 C. butter	1 tsp. vanilla
2 eggs	Powdered sugar, optional

Preheat waffle iron. In a double boiler over low heat, place unsweetened chocolate squares. Heat, stirring occasionally, until chocolate is melted. In a medium bowl, cream together brown sugar and butter. Add melted chocolate and mix well. Stir in eggs, flour, baking powder, salt and vanilla. Mix until well combined. Lightly spray waffle iron with non-stick cooking spray. Drop about 1 tablespoon dough into each section of the waffle iron. Bake cookies until lightly browned, being careful not to burn. Let cookies cool on a wire rack. If desired, dust with powdered sugar.

Chocolate Dipped Mocha Rounds

Makes 5 dozen

2 (1 oz.) squares unsweetened
   chocolate
1/2 C. butter
1/2 C. plus 3 T. shortening,
   divided
1/2 C. sugar
1/2 C. brown sugar

1 T. instant coffee granules
1 T. water
1 egg
2 C. flour
1 tsp. cinnamon
1/4 tsp. salt
1 1/2 C. chocolate chips

In a heavy saucepan over medium heat, melt unsweetened chocolate squares. Remove from heat and let cool slightly. In a large mixing bowl, combine butter and 1/2 cup shortening until softened. Add sugar and brown sugar and beat until fluffy. In a small bowl, combine instant coffee granules and water, mixing until coffee is dissolved. Add coffee mixture, melted chocolate and egg to butter mixture. Stir in flour, cinnamon and salt, mixing until well combined. Cover dough and chill in refrigerator for about 1 hour. Shape dough into two 7" logs. Wrap logs in plastic wrap and chill in refrigerator for an additional 6 hours or overnight. Preheat oven to 350°. Cut logs into 1/4" thick slices and place on ungreased baking sheets. Bake for 10 to 12 minutes. Set cookies on wire racks to cool. In a double boiler over low heat, combine chocolate chips and remaining 3 tablespoons shortening. Heat, stirring occasionally, until melted. Dip each cookie half way into the melted chocolate mixture. Place dipped cookies on waxed paper until set.

Easy Chocolate Butterscotch Rounds

Makes 2 dozen

1 (18 1/4 oz.) pkg. chocolate
    cake mix
1/2 C. vegetable oil

2 eggs
2 C. butterscotch chips

Preheat oven to 350°. Lightly grease baking sheets and set aside. In a large bowl, combine chocolate cake mix, vegetable oil and eggs. Mix well and fold in butterscotch chips. Drop dough by tablespoonfuls onto prepared baking sheets. Bake in oven for 8 to 10 minutes or until center of cookies are set. Let cookies cool slightly on baking sheets before removing to wire racks.

All I really need is love, but a little chocolate now and then doesn't hurt!

Chocolate Macaroons

Makes 3 dozen

1 1/2 C. chocolate chips
3 eggs whites
Pinch of salt
3/4 C. sugar

1 tsp. vanilla
2 1/4 C. shredded coconut
1/2 C. chopped walnuts

    Preheat oven to 325°. Lightly grease baking sheets and set aside. In a double boiler over low heat, place chocolate chips. Remove from heat and let cool slightly. In a large mixing bowl, beat egg whites until foamy. Slowly add salt and sugar, a little at a time, until soft peaks form. Stir in vanilla. Fold in melted chocolate, shredded coconut and chopped walnuts. Drop dough by teaspoonfuls 2" apart onto prepared baking sheets. Bake in oven for 10 to 12 minutes. Cookies should be soft in the center. Let cookies cool slightly on baking sheets before removing to wire racks.

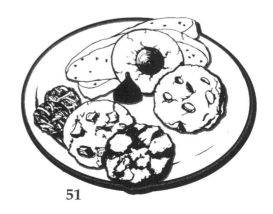

Crispy Chocolates

Makes 1 dozen

1 T. butter, softened
1 egg white
1/4 C. sugar
1 tsp. vanilla
2 1/2 T. flour
1 T. cocoa powder

Pinch of salt
1/2 (1 oz.) square
    unsweetened chocolate,
    grated
1/3 C. powdered sugar,
    optional

Preheat oven to 300°. Lightly grease baking sheets and set aside. In a small saucepan over medium heat, place butter until lightly browned. Transfer butter to a medium bowl. Add egg white, sugar and vanilla. In a separate bowl, combine flour, cocoa powder and salt. Add flour mixture to butter mixture, mixing until well combined. Fold in grated chocolate. Drop dough by teaspoonfuls 2" apart on prepared baking sheets. Bake in oven for 12 to 15 minutes. Let cookies cool slightly onto baking sheets before removing to wire racks. If desired, dust with powdered sugar.

Exercise is a dirty word...
Every time I hear, I wash my
mouth out with chocolate.

Granola Chocolate Cookies

Makes 4 dozen

1 C. butter, softened
3/4 C. brown sugar
3/4 C. sugar
1 egg
1 tsp. vanilla
1 1/2 C. flour

1 tsp. salt
1 tsp. baking soda
1 3/4 C. granola
1 C. chocolate chips
1/2 C. chopped, unsalted
     dry roasted peanuts

     Preheat oven to 375°. Lightly grease baking sheets and set aside. In a medium bowl, cream together butter, brown sugar and sugar. Add egg and vanilla and mix well. In a separate bowl, combine flour, salt and baking soda. Add flour mixture to butter mixture and mix well. Fold in granola, chocolate chips and peanuts. Drop dough by heaping teaspoonfuls 2" apart onto prepared baking sheets. Bake in oven for 12 to 15 minutes, until cookies are lightly browned around edges. Remove cookies to wire racks to cool.

Peanut Butter Chocolate Drop Cookies

Makes 4 dozen

2 (1 oz.) squares
    unsweetened chocolate
1 C. plus 3 T. flour, divided
1/2 C. sugar
1/2 C. shortening
1 egg

1 tsp. salt
1 tsp. vanilla
1/2 C. brown sugar
1/4 C. peanut butter
2 T. butter, softened

Preheat oven to 325°. Lightly grease baking sheets and set aside. In a double boiler over medium heat, place unsweetened chocolate squares. Heat, stirring frequently, until melted. In a large mixing bowl, combine melted chocolate, 1 cup flour, sugar, shortening, egg, salt and vanilla. In a small bowl, combine remaining 3 tablespoons flour, brown sugar, peanut butter and butter. Mixture should be crumbly. Drop chocolate dough mixture by teaspoonfuls 1" apart onto prepared baking sheets. Top each cookie with 1/2 teaspoon of the peanut butter dough mixture. Dip a fork into flour and gently press fork across the top of each cookie. Bake in oven for 12 minutes, or until firm. Remove cookies to wire racks to cool.

Chewy Chocolate & Cinnamon Cookies

Makes 3 to 4 dozen

6 T. butter or margarine,
   softened
2/3 C. brown sugar
1/4 C. plus 3 T. sugar,
   divided
1 egg

1 tsp. baking soda
1/4 C. light corn syrup
1 tsp. vanilla
1 1/2 C. flour
1/3 C. cocoa powder
1/4 to 1/2 tsp. cinnamon

Preheat oven to 350°. Lightly grease baking sheets and set aside. In a large mixing bowl, beat butter until creamy. Add brown sugar and 3 tablespoons sugar and mix at medium speed until blended. Add egg, baking soda, corn syrup and vanilla. Reduce speed to low and mix until well blended. In a small bowl, combine flour and cocoa powder. Add flour mixture to butter mixture. If batter becomes too thick, use a wooden spoon to mix ingredients. Shape dough into 1" balls. In a small bowl, combine remaining 1/4 cup sugar and cinnamon. Roll balls in sugar and cinnamon mixture and set 2" apart on prepared baking sheets. Bake in oven for 9 to 10 minutes, or until cookies are set. Top of cookies will crack slightly. Remove cookies to wire racks to cool.

White Chocolate Macadamia Cookies

Makes 2 dozen

1/2 C. butter, softened
1/2 C. shortening
3/4 C. sugar
1/2 C. brown sugar
1 egg
2 tsp. vanilla
1 3/4 C. flour

1 tsp. baking soda
1/2 tsp. salt
10 (1 oz.) squares white
    chocolate, chopped
1/2 C. chopped macadamia
    nuts, toasted*

In a large mixing bowl, cream together butter and shortening. Beat at medium speed and gradually add sugar and brown sugar. Beat in egg and vanilla. In a medium bowl, combine flour, baking soda and salt. Add flour mixture to butter mixture and blend well. Using a wooden spoon, fold in chopped white chocolate and toasted macadamia nuts. Cover dough and chill in refrigerator for 1 hour. Preheat oven to 350°. Lightly grease baking sheets. Drop dough by heaping tablespoonfuls 3" apart onto prepared baking sheets. Bake in oven for 12 to 14 minutes. Cookies will be soft. Let cookies cool slightly on baking sheets before removing to wire racks.

* To toast, place macadamia nuts in a single layer on a baking sheet. Bake at 350° for approximately 10 minutes or until macadamia nuts are golden brown.

Peanut Butter Cup Cookies

Makes 3 1/2 dozen

1 (13 oz.) pkg. Reese's
    miniature peanut
    butter cups
1/2 C. butter or margarine,
    softened
1/2 C. creamy peanut butter
1/2 C. brown sugar

1/4 C. sugar
1 egg
1 2/3 C. flour
1 tsp. baking soda
1 C. crushed corn flakes
1 egg white
1 T. water

Preheat oven to 375°. Remove wrappers from peanut butter cups and set aside. Lightly grease baking sheets and set aside. In a large bowl, combine butter, peanut butter, brown sugar and sugar, mixing until lightened and fluffy. Add egg and mix well. In a separate bowl, combine flour and baking soda. Add flour mixture to butter mixture. Mix well. Shape dough into 1" balls. In a shallow bowl, place crushed corn flakes. In a small bowl, whisk together egg white and water, beating until foamy. Roll balls in egg white mixture and then in crushed corn flakes. Place balls 2" apart on prepared baking sheets. Press thumb in the center of each ball to make an indentation. Bake in oven for 8 to 10 minutes, until cookies are set. Remove from oven and immediately press one peanut butter cup in the indentation in each cookie. Let cookies cool slightly on baking sheets before removing to wire racks.

Chocolate Scotcheroos

Makes 4 dozen

1 C. sugar
1 C. light corn syrup
1 C. peanut butter

6 C. crispy rice cereal
1 C. chocolate chips
1 C. butterscotch chips

Grease a 9x13" baking dish and set aside. In a medium saucepan over medium heat, combine sugar and corn syrup and bring to a rolling boil. Remove from heat and stir in peanut butter. Add crispy rice cereal and stir until fully coated. Press mixture into prepared pan. In a double boiler over medium heat, combine chocolate chips and butterscotch chips. Heat, stirring occasionally, until melted. Spread melted chocolate mixture over ingredients in baking dish. Chill in refrigerator until set. Cut into bars.

Almond Fudge Topped Shortbread

Makes 2 to 3 dozen

1 C. butter or margarine,
softened
1/2 C. powdered sugar
1/4 tsp. salt
1 1/4 C. flour
2 C. chocolate chips

1 (14 oz.) can sweetened
condensed milk
1/2 tsp. almond extract
1/2 C. sliced almonds,
toasted*

Preheat oven to 350°. Grease a 9x13" baking dish and set aside. In a large mixing bowl, beat butter, powdered sugar and salt at low speed until blended. Add flour and mix until well combined. Flour hands and press mixture into prepared pan. Bake in oven for 20 minutes or until lightly browned. In a heavy saucepan over low heat, combine chocolate chips and sweetened condensed milk. Heat, stirring constantly, until chocolate is melted. Stir in almond extract and spread melted chocolate mixture over baked shortbread. Sprinkle with toasted almonds. Let cool slightly and chill in refrigerator until chocolate is set, about 3 hours. Cut into bars.

* To toast, place sliced almonds in a single layer on a baking sheet. Bake at 350° for approximately 10 minutes or until sliced almonds are golden brown.

White Chocolate Brownies

Makes 2 dozen

6 (1 oz.) squares white
    chocolate, chopped
3/4 C. sugar
1/2 C. butter
2 eggs
1 1/2 tsp. vanilla
1 C. flour

1/2 tsp. baking powder
Pinch of salt
6 (1 oz.) squares semi-sweet
    or bittersweet chocolate,
    chopped
1/2 C. chopped walnuts

Preheat oven to 350°. Lightly grease a 7x11" baking dish and set aside. In a large glass measuring cup or bowl, place chopped white chocolate, sugar and butter. Place in microwave on high for 1 1/2 minutes, until mixture is melted. Stir until smooth. Using a wire whisk, blend in eggs and vanilla. Add flour, baking powder and salt and stir until well mixed. Fold in chopped chocolate and chopped walnuts. Spread mixture into prepared pan. Bake in oven for 20 to 25 minutes or until golden brown, being careful not to overbake. Let cool slightly before cutting into bars.

Simply put...everyone has
a price, mine is chocolate!

Mudslide Brownies

Makes 2 dozen

2 C. flour
1/2 tsp. baking powder
1/2 tsp. salt
2/3 C. butter
4 (1 oz.) squares unsweetened
    chocolate, chopped
3 eggs

1 1/2 C. sugar
4 T. Kahlua
2 T. Irish cream liqueur
1 T. vodka
3/4 C. coarsely chopped
    walnuts, optional
Kahlua Glaze

Preheat oven to 350°. Lightly grease a 9x13" baking dish and set aside. Into a medium bowl, sift flour, baking powder and salt. In a small saucepan over low heat, combine butter and chopped chocolate, mixing until chocolate is melted. Remove from heat and let cool slightly. In a large bowl, combine melted chocolate mixture, flour mixture, eggs, sugar, Kahlua, Irish cream liqueur and vodka. If desired, fold in chopped walnuts. Pour mixture into prepared pan. Bake in oven for 25 minutes. Remove from oven and let cool in pan. Spread Kahlua Glaze over brownies. Cut into bars.

Kahlua Glaze

1 1/4 C. powdered sugar

3 T. Kahlua

In a small bowl, combine powdered sugar and Kahlua, mixing until a glaze forms. Spread over cooled Mudslide Brownies.

Blonde Brownies

Makes 3 dozen

1 C. shortening
2 eggs
1 1/2 C. brown sugar
2 T. milk
1 tsp. vanilla

2 C. flour
1 tsp. baking powder
1/4 tsp. baking soda
1/4 tsp. salt
1 C. chocolate chips

Preheat oven to 350°. Grease a 9x13" baking dish and set aside. In a large bowl, cream together shortening, eggs and brown sugar. Add milk and vanilla and mix well. Gradually stir in flour, baking powder, baking soda and salt. Stir until well blended. Fold in chocolate chips, mixing until well incorporated. Spread dough into prepared pan. Bake in oven for 25 to 30 minutes. Let cool slightly before cutting into bars.

I don't understand why so many chocolate lovers complain about the calories in chocolate. All true chocoholics know that it is a vegetable. Chocolate comes from the cocoa bean and beans are veggies!

Double Delicious Cookie Bars

Makes 2 to 3 dozen

1/2 C. butter or margarine
1 1/2 C. graham cracker
   crumbs
1 (14 oz.) can sweetened
   condensed milk

1 C. peanut butter chips
3 C. chocolate chips, divided
1 1/2 tsp. vegetable
   shortening

Preheat oven to 350°. In a 9x13" baking dish, place butter. Place pan in oven until butter is melted. Sprinkle graham cracker crumbs over melted butter and press down slightly. Pour sweetened condensed milk over graham cracker crumbs. Top with peanut butter chips and 2 cups chocolate chips. Press down on chips evenly and firmly. Bake in oven for 25 to 30 minutes, until bars are lightly browned. Let cool completely in pan. In a small microwave safe bowl, combine remaining 1 cup chocolate chips and vegetable shortening. Microwave on high for 1 to 1 1/2 minutes, until melted. Stir and drizzle melted chocolate over cooled bars. Cut into bars.

Chocolate Cherry Biscotti

Makes 3 dozen

1/2 C. butter, softened
3/4 C. sugar
3 eggs
2 tsp. almond extract
3 C. flour
2 tsp. baking powder

1/2 C. chopped candied
cherries
1/2 C. miniature
chocolate chips
1/2 C. chopped white
chocolate

Preheat oven to 350°. Grease a large baking sheet and set aside. In a large bowl, cream together butter and sugar until smooth. Add eggs, one at a time, mixing well after each addition. Add almond extract, flour and baking powder and stir just until blended. Fold in candied cherries and chocolate chips. Lightly flour hands and divide dough into two parts. Shape each part into a 10" loaf. Place loaves 5" apart on prepared baking sheet. Flatten each loaf to 3" in width. Bake for 20 to 25 minutes, or until light golden brown. Remove to wire racks and let cool for 10 minutes. Using a serrated knife, cut each loaf into 1/2" slices. Arrange slices, cut side down, on ungreased baking sheets. Bake for 8 to 10 minutes, or until bottoms begin to brown. Turn and bake for an additional 5 minutes, or until browned and crisp. Remove from oven and let cool completely. In a double boiler over medium heat, melt white chocolate, stirring until smooth. Drizzle white chocolate over cooled biscotti.

*When the going gets tough,
the tough eat chocolate.*

Almond Chocolate Biscotti

Makes 3 dozen

2 C. flour
1/2 tsp. baking soda
1/2 tsp. baking powder
1/8 tsp. salt
7/8 C. sugar
1 1/2 C. blanched whole
   almonds, toasted*

2 C. chocolate chips
2 eggs
1 tsp. vanilla
2 T. whiskey

Preheat oven to 375°. Line baking sheets with aluminum foil and set aside. Into a medium bowl, sift flour, baking soda, baking powder and salt. Add sugar and mix well. Place half of the flour mixture into a blender or food processor. Add 1/2 cup toasted almonds and blend for about 30 seconds. Add mixture to remaining flour mixture. Stir in remaining 1 cup toasted almonds and chocolate chips and mix well. In a separate bowl, lightly beat eggs and add vanilla and whiskey. Pour egg mixture into dry ingredients and stir until moistened. Divide dough into four equal parts. Lightly wet hands under cold water and form each part into a 9" log, 2" wide and 1/2" thick. Place logs on baking sheets and bake in oven for 25 minutes. Remove logs from baking sheets and let cool slightly. Reduce oven temperature to 275°. Using a serrated knife, slice logs into 1/2" thick slices. Arrange slices, cut side down, on ungreased baking sheets. Bake for 25 to 30 minutes. Remove from oven and let cool completely.

* To toast, place blanched almonds in a single layer on a baking sheet. Bake at 350° for approximately 10 minutes or until almonds are golden brown.

Double Chocolate Biscotti

Makes 3 dozen

1/2 C. butter, softened
2/3 C. sugar
1/4 C. cocoa powder
2 tsp. baking powder
2 eggs

1 3/4 C. flour
4 (1 oz.) squares white
    chocolate, chopped
3/4 C. chocolate chips

In a large mixing bowl, beat butter and sugar at medium speed until lightened. Gradually add cocoa powder and baking powder, beating for 2 minutes. Add eggs, one at a time, beating well after each addition. Stir in flour by hand. Using a wooden spoon, fold in chopped white chocolate and chocolate chips. Cover dough and chill in refrigerator for 10 minutes. Preheat oven to 375°. Lightly grease a baking sheet. Divide dough into two equal parts. Roll each part into a 9" log. Place logs 4" apart on prepared baking sheet. Flatten each loaf to 3" in width. Bake for 20 to 25 minutes, or until a toothpick inserted in center of logs comes out clean. Remove to wire racks and let cool for 10 minutes. Reduce oven temperature to 325°. Using a serrated knife, cut each loaf into 1/2" thick slices. Arrange slices, cut side down, on ungreased baking sheets. Bake for 9 minutes. Turn and bake for an additional 7 to 9 minutes, or until browned and crisp. Remove from oven and let cool completely.

Cakes

Chocolate Orange Marble Chiffon Cake

Makes 12 to 16 servings

1/3 C. cocoa powder
1/4 C. hot water
1 1/2 C. plus 3 T. sugar,
    divided
1/2 C. plus 2 T. vegetable oil,
    divided
2 1/4 C. flour
3 tsp. baking powder

1 tsp. salt
3/4 C. cold water
7 egg yolks
1 C. egg whites
1/2 tsp. cream of tartar
1 T. grated orange peel
Orange Glaze, optional

Preheat oven to 325°. Lightly grease a 10" tube pan. In a medium bowl, combine cocoa powder and hot water. Stir in 3 tablespoons sugar and 2 tablespoons vegetable oil and set aside. In a large bowl, combine flour, remaining 1 1/2 cups sugar, baking powder and salt. Mix well and add cold water, remaining 1/2 cup vegetable oil and egg yolks. Stir well until mixture is smooth. In a large mixing bowl, beat egg whites and cream of tartar at high speed until stiff peaks form. Slowly pour egg yolk mixture into egg whites, mixing until just blended. Remove 2 cups of batter and add to cocoa powder mixture. Mix grated orange peel into the white batter. Spoon half of the white batter into prepared tube pan. Drop half of the chocolate batter in spoonfuls over white batter. Cover with remaining white batter and top with spoonfuls of remaining chocolate batter. Using a knife, gently swirl cake batters together to achieve a marbled effect. Bake in oven for 1 hour and 15 minutes or until a toothpick inserted in cake comes out clean. Immediately invert cake onto a wire rack and let cool. Carefully remove cake from pan. If desired, top with Orange Glaze.

Orange Glaze

1/3 C. butter
2 C. powdered sugar

2 to 3 T. orange juice
1/2 tsp. grated orange peel

In a medium saucepan over low heat, melt butter. Remove from heat and stir in powdered sugar, orange juice and grated orange peel, beating until smooth. Drizzle over Chocolate Orange Marble Chiffon Cake.

Researchers have discovered that chocolate produces some of the same reactions in the brain as marijuana. The researchers also discovered other similarities between the two, but can't remember what they are. ~ Matt Lauer

Cake Squares with Eggnog Sauce

Makes 12 to 15 servings

1 C. buttermilk	2 C. sugar
1 1/2 tsp. baking soda	2 eggs
3/4 C. cocoa powder	1 tsp. vanilla
3/4 C. boiling water	1/8 tsp. salt
1/4 C. butter or margarine, softened	1 3/4 C. flour
1/4 C. shortening	Powdered sugar
	Eggnog Sauce

Preheat oven to 350°. Grease and flour a 9x13" baking dish and set aside. In a medium bowl, combine buttermilk and baking soda. Mix well and set aside. In a small bowl, combine cocoa powder and boiling water. Mix well and set aside. In a large mixing bowl, beat together butter, shortening and sugar until creamy. Add eggs, vanilla and salt and mix well. Alternating, add flour and buttermilk mixture to butter mixture, mixing until well blended. Stir in cocoa powder mixture and pour batter into prepared pan. Bake in oven for 40 to 45 minutes or until a toothpick inserted in center of cake comes out clean. Remove from oven and let cool completely. Sprinkle with powdered sugar. Cut into squares and serve with Eggnog Sauce.

Eggnog Sauce

1 T. cornstarch
2 T. cold water
1 1/3 C. milk
1/4 C. sugar

3 egg yolks, beaten
1/4 tsp. brandy extract
1/4 tsp. vanilla
Pinch of nutmeg

In a medium saucepan over medium heat, combine cornstarch and water, mixing until smooth. Add milk, sugar and beaten egg yolks. Beat with a wire whisk until blended. Cook, stirring constantly, until thickened. Remove from heat and stir in brandy extract and vanilla. Let cool completely and sprinkle with nutmeg. Pour over Cake Squares.

Caramels are only a fad.
Chocolate is a permanent thing.
~ Milton Snavely Hershey

Chocolate Banana Cake

Makes 14 servings

1 (18 1/4 oz.) pkg. devil's
    food cake mix
1 C. mashed bananas

1/3 C. vegetable oil
3 eggs
Frosting, optional

Preheat oven to 350°. Grease and flour a 9x13" baking dish and set aside. In a large mixing bowl, combine cake mix, mashed bananas, vegetable oil and eggs at low speed for 30 seconds. Increase speed to medium and beat for an additional 2 minutes. Pour batter into prepared pan. Bake in oven for 33 to 36 minutes or until a toothpick inserted in center of cake comes out clean. Let cake cool completely. If desired, cake can be frosted.

If not for chocolate, there would be no need for control top pantyhose. An entire garment industry would be devastated.

Rich Raspberry Chocolate Cake

Makes 12 servings

6 (1 oz.) squares
    unsweetened chocolate
12 (1 oz.) squares semi-sweet
    chocolate, divided
7 eggs, separated
1 C. butter, softened
2 C. sugar, divided

1 1/2 tsp. vanilla
1 C. flour
3/4 C. heavy whipping cream
1 (4 oz.) pkg. frozen raspberries,
    thawed
3 T. seedless raspberry
    preserves

Preheat oven to 300°. Line the bottoms of two 9" cake pans with waxed paper and set aside. In a double boiler over medium heat, place unsweetened chocolate squares and 6 semi-sweet chocolate squares. Heat until melted and stir in egg yolks. Remove from heat and let cool. In a large bowl, cream together butter, 1 1/2 cups sugar and vanilla. Add melted chocolate mixture and mix until smooth. Add flour and mix just until blended. In a separate bowl, beat egg whites until foamy. Gradually add remaining 1/2 cup sugar and beat until soft peaks form. Fold egg white mixture into chocolate mixture. Pour batter into prepared pans. Bake in oven for 45 minutes or until a toothpick inserted in center of cakes comes out clean. Let cakes cool completely. To make frosting, in a medium saucepan over medium heat, bring heavy cream to a boil. Chop remaining 6 semi-sweet chocolate squares and add to boiling cream. Remove saucepan from heat and stir until smooth. Pour mixture into a bowl and cover tightly. Chill in refrigerator until thickened. To make filling, drain thawed raspberries and set in a medium bowl. Mix with raspberry preserves. To assemble cake, set one cake layer on serving platter. Spread with raspberry filling and top with remaining cake layer. Spread chocolate frosting over top and sides of cake.

Wacky Peanut Butter & Chocolate Cake

Makes 18 servings

3 C. flour
2 tsp. baking soda
1 tsp. salt
6 T. cocoa powder
2 C. sugar
10 T. plus 1/4 C. butter, melted

2 tsp. white vinegar
2 C. warm water
1/4 C. peanut butter
1 C. brown sugar
1/4 C. milk

Preheat oven to 350°. Lightly grease a 9x13" baking dish and set aside. Into a large bowl, sift flour, baking soda, salt, cocoa powder and sugar. Add 10 tablespoons melted butter, vinegar and warm water and mix well. Pour batter into prepared pan. Bake in oven for 30 to 35 minutes. Remove cake from oven and let cool. In a medium bowl, cream together peanut butter, brown sugar, milk and remaining 1/4 cup butter. Spread mixture over cooled cake. Preheat broiler. Set cake under broiler for a few seconds, until topping is browned and bubbly.

Everything I eat should contain either garlic or chocolate, but rarely both!

Chocolate Ice Cream Cake

Makes 10 to 12 servings

2 eggs, separated
1 1/2 C. sugar, divided
1 1/4 C. flour
1/2 C. cocoa powder
3/4 tsp. baking soda
1/2 tsp. salt

1/2 C. vegetable oil
1 C. buttermilk
1 gallon ice cream,
    any kind, softened
3/4 C. whipped topping

Preheat oven to 350°. Grease and flour three 9" round cake pans and set aside. In a small mixing bowl, beat egg whites at low speed until foamy and gradually add 1/2 cup sugar, beating until stiff peaks form. In a large bowl, combine flour, remaining 1 cup sugar, cocoa powder, baking soda and salt. Add vegetable oil, buttermilk and egg yolks. Mix well and gently fold in egg white mixture. Pour batter evenly into prepared pans. Bake in oven for 18 to 20 minutes, or until a toothpick inserted in center of cakes comes out clean. Let cakes cool in pans for 5 minutes before removing from cake pans to wire racks. Let cakes cool completely and wrap each layer in aluminum foil. Place wrapped cake layers in freezer for several hours. To prepare ice cream layers, line two 9" round cake pans with aluminum foil. Spread half of the softened ice cream into each cake pan. Cover pans tightly and place in freezer until firm. To assemble cake, unwrap each cake layer. Place one cake layer on serving platter. Top with one ice cream layer and peel off aluminum foil. Top with another cake layer, remaining ice cream layer and final cake layer. Wrap entire cake and return to freezer until ready to serve. Before serving, garnish the top of the cake with whipped topping.

Apple Pie Chocolate Brownie Cake

Makes 8 to 10 servings

1 C. flour
2/3 C. sugar
1/4 C. cocoa powder
1 tsp. baking powder
1/2 tsp. salt
3/4 C. water

2/3 C. shortening
1 egg
1 tsp. vanilla
Apple Topping
Whipped topping or
    ice cream, optional

Preheat oven to 375°. Grease and flour a 9" square pan. In a medium bowl, combine flour, sugar, cocoa powder, baking powder and salt. Add water, shortening, egg and vanilla and beat until well blended and smooth. Spread mixture into prepared pan. Carefully spoon Apple Topping over batter in pan, to within 1/2" from the edges of the pan. Do not stir. Bake in oven for 35 to 40 minutes or until cake is set. Remove from oven and let cool completely. Cut into squares. If desired, serve with whipped topping or ice cream.

Apple Topping

1 (20 oz.) can apple
    pie filling
1/2 tsp. lemon juice

1/2 tsp. cinnamon

In a small bowl, combine apple pie filling, lemon juice and cinnamon. Mix until well incorporated.

Black Bottom Cupcakes

Makes 2 dozen

1 (8 oz.) pkg. cream cheese, softened
1 egg
1 1/3 C. sugar, divided
1/2 tsp. plus 1/8 tsp. salt, divided
1 C. miniature chocolate chips

1 1/2 C. flour
1/4 C. cocoa powder
1 tsp. baking soda
1 C. water
1/3 C. vegetable oil
1 T. cider vinegar
1 tsp. vanilla

Preheat oven to 350°. Line 2 1/2" muffin cups with paper liners. In a medium bowl, combine cream cheese, egg, 1/3 cup sugar and 1/8 teaspoon salt. Mix until lightened and fluffy. Add miniature chocolate chips, stir until combined and set aside. In a large bowl, combine flour, remaining 1 cup sugar, cocoa powder, baking soda and remaining 1/2 teaspoon salt. Form a well in the center of the dry ingredients and add water, vegetable oil, vinegar and vanilla. Mix until fully blended. Fill prepared muffin cups 1/3 full with batter. Top the batter in each muffin cup with a dollop of the cream cheese mixture. Bake in oven for 25 to 30 minutes. Remove from heat and let cool on a wire rack.

So Simple Crazy Chocolate Cake

Makes 18 servings

3 C. flour
2 C. sugar
5/8 C. cocoa powder
1 tsp. salt
2 tsp. baking soda

1 tsp. vanilla
2 C. cold water
2 tsp. white vinegar
2/3 C. vegetable oil
Frosting, optional

Preheat oven to 350°. In a 9x13" baking dish, combine flour, sugar, cocoa powder, salt, baking soda, vanilla, cold water, vinegar and vegetable oil. Mix until well blended. Bake in oven for 35 minutes. Remove from oven and let cool completely. If desired, frost with frosting.

*Man cannot live on chocolate
alone; but woman sure can.*

Chocolate-Flecked Spice Cake

Makes 10 servings

1/2 C. butter, softened
1 C. sugar
2 eggs
1 C. flour
Pinch of ground cloves

1 tsp. cinnamon
1/2 tsp. baking soda
1/2 C. buttermilk
1 (1 oz.) square semi-sweet
   chocolate, grated

Preheat oven to 350°. Lightly grease and flour an 8" round pan. In a large bowl, cream together butter and sugar. Add eggs, one at a time, beating well after each addition. Into a separate bowl, sift flour, ground cloves and cinnamon. Add flour mixture to butter mixture. In a small bowl, combine baking soda and buttermilk, stirring until baking soda is dissolved. Add buttermilk mixture to butter mixture. Fold in grated chocolate. Pour batter into prepared cake pan. Bake in oven for 20 minutes, or until a toothpick inserted in center of cake comes out clean. Remove from oven and let cool completely.

I have a theory that chocolate slows down the aging process...it may not be true, but do I dare take the chance?

Chocolate Chip Crater Cake

Makes 9 servings

2 C. Bisquick baking mix
1 egg
2/3 C. milk
1/4 C. sugar

1 tsp. vanilla
1 C. chocolate chips
Topping Mix

Preheat oven to 350°. Grease an 8" square pan and set aside. In a large mixing bowl, combine baking mix, egg, milk, sugar and vanilla. Beat at low speed until mixture is moistened. Increase speed to medium and beat for an additional 2 minutes, until smooth. Pour half of the batter into prepared pan. Sprinkle chocolate chips over batter. Pour remaining half of the batter over chocolate chips. Sprinkle Topping Mix over batter. Bake in oven for 25 to 30 minutes or until a toothpick inserted in center of cake comes out clean. Remove from oven and let cool completely.

Topping Mix

1/4 C. sugar
1/4 C. brown sugar
1/4 C. Bisquick baking mix

1/4 C. butter or margarine,
  softened
1 tsp. cinnamon

In a medium bowl, combine sugar, brown sugar, baking mix, butter and cinnamon. Blend until mixture resembles coarse crumbs.

Gooey Chocolate Cakes

Makes 6 cakes

7 (1 oz.) squares bittersweet
   chocolate, finely chopped
14 T. butter
4 eggs

4 egg yolks
1 1/2 C. powdered sugar
3/4 C. flour

Preheat oven to 425°. Lightly spray six 3" muffin cups with nonstick cooking spray. In a double boiler over simmering water, place chopped chocolate and butter. Heat, stirring occasionally, until completely melted. Remove from heat and add eggs and egg yolks, stirring lightly with a whisk. Add powdered sugar and flour and stir until completely incorporated. Pour batter into prepared muffin cups. Bake in oven for 7 minutes. Remove from oven and serve immediately. Cake may appear to be under-baked.

Cherry Chocolate Upside-Down Cake

Makes 24 servings

1 (21 oz.) can cherry pie
   filling
2 1/4 C. flour
1 1/2 C. sugar
3/4 C. cocoa powder
1 1/2 tsp. baking soda

3/4 tsp. salt
1 1/2 C. water
1/2 C. vegetable oil
1/4 C. white vinegar
1/2 tsp. vanilla

Preheat oven to 350°. Spread cherry pie filling evenly in the bottom of a greased 9x13" pan. In a large bowl, combine flour, sugar, cocoa powder, baking soda and salt. In a medium bowl, combine water, vegetable oil, vinegar and vanilla. Pour water mixture into flour mixture and stir just until moistened. Pour batter evenly over cherry pie filling in pan. Bake in oven for 30 to 35 minutes, until a toothpick inserted in center of cake comes out clean. Remove from oven and let cool completely.

*If it ain't chocolate,
it ain't breakfast.*

Sour Cream Chocolate Cake

Makes 18 servings

2 eggs
2 T. butter, melted
1 1/2 C. sour cream
3 1/4 C. sugar, divided
2 C. flour
4 T. cocoa powder
1/2 tsp. salt, divided
2 tsp. vanilla, divided

2 tsp. baking soda
1/4 C. hot water
1/4 C. light corn syrup
1/2 C. milk
1/2 C. shortening
2 (1 oz.) squares
  unsweetened chocolate,
  chopped

Preheat oven to 350°. Lightly grease and flour a 9x13" baking dish. In a large bowl, beat eggs. Add melted butter and sour cream and mix well. Into a separate bowl, sift 1 1/4 cups sugar, flour, cocoa powder and 1/4 teaspoon salt. Add flour mixture to egg mixture and mix until smooth. Add vanilla and mix well. In a small bowl, combine baking soda and hot water. Mix until baking soda is dissolved and add to egg mixture. Pour batter into prepared baking dish. Bake in oven for 35 minutes, or until a toothpick inserted in center of cake comes out clean. To make frosting, in a small saucepan over low heat, combine remaining 2 cups sugar, corn syrup, milk, shortening, unsweetened chocolate and remaining 1/4 teaspoon salt. Heat, stirring frequently, until chocolate is melted. Bring mixture to a boil for 1 minute. Remove from heat and stir in remaining 1 teaspoon vanilla, mixing until smooth. Spread frosting over cooled cake.

*I could give up chocolate...
but I'm not a quitter.*

Oatmeal Chocolate Chip Cake

Makes 24 servings

1 3/4 C. boiling water	1 3/4 C. flour
1 C. old fashioned oats	1 tsp. baking soda
1 C. brown sugar	1 T. cocoa powder
1 C. sugar	1/2 tsp. salt
1/2 C. butter	1 C. chocolate chips
2 eggs	1/2 C. chopped walnuts

Preheat oven to 350°. Lightly grease and flour a 10x15" jellyroll pan. In a large bowl, combine boiling water and oats. Mix and let sit for 10 minutes. Add brown sugar, sugar, butter and eggs. Mix well and add flour, baking soda, cocoa powder and salt. Mix well and pour into prepared pan. Sprinkle chocolate chips and chopped walnuts over batter. Bake in oven for 20 minutes. Remove from oven and let cool slightly before cutting into bars.

Put "eat chocolate" at the top of your list of things to do today. That way, at least you will get one thing done.

Zucchini Chocolate Cake

Makes 18 servings

1/2 C. butter, softened
1/2 C. vegetable oil
1 3/4 C. sugar
2 eggs
1/2 C. buttermilk
1 tsp. vanilla
2 C. flour
1 tsp. baking soda

1/2 tsp. cinnamon
1/2 tsp. ground cloves
1/2 tsp. salt
4 T. cocoa powder
2 1/2 C. grated zucchini
1/4 C. ground walnuts
1/4 C. chocolate chips

Preheat oven to 325°. Grease and flour a 9x13″ baking dish and set aside. In a large bowl, cream together butter, vegetable oil and sugar. Add eggs, buttermilk and vanilla and mix well. Into a separate bowl, sift flour, baking soda, cinnamon, ground cloves, salt and cocoa powder. Add dry ingredients to butter mixture and mix well. Fold in grated zucchini and spread mixture into prepared pan. Sprinkle ground walnuts and chocolate chips over cake. Bake in oven for 45 minutes. Remove from oven and let cool before cutting into squares.

Chocolate: Here today...Gone Today!

Glazed Chocolate Citrus Poppy Seed Cake

Makes 12 servings

1 (18 oz.) pkg. lemon
   cake mix
1/3 C. poppy seeds
1/3 C. milk
3 eggs

1 (8 oz.) container plain
   yogurt
1 tsp. grated lemon peel
Chocolate Citrus Glaze

Preheat oven to 350°. Grease and flour a 12-cup fluted tube pan or 10" tube pan and set aside. In a large bowl, combine lemon cake mix, poppy seeds, milk, eggs, plain yogurt and grated lemon peel. Mix well and pour batter into prepared pan. Bake in oven for 40 to 45 minutes or until a toothpick inserted in center of cake comes out clean. Remove from oven and let cool in pan for 20 minutes. Remove from pan to a wire rack. Spoon Chocolate Citrus Glaze over cake and allow glaze to run down sides of cake.

Chocolate Citrus Glaze

2 T. butter or margarine
2 T. cocoa powder
2 T. water

1 T. Triple Sec, optional
1/2 tsp. orange extract
1 1/4 to 1 1/2 C. powdered sugar

In a small saucepan over medium heat, melt butter. Using a wire whisk, stir in cocoa powder and water, stirring until mixture slightly thickens. Remove from heat and stir in Triple Sec, orange extract and powdered sugar. Stir until smooth and drizzle over Citrus Poppy Seed Cake.

S'mores Cupcakes

Makes 2 dozen

1 (18 1/4 oz.) pkg. French
    vanilla cake mix
1/2 C. plus 2 T. graham
    cracker crumbs, divided
1 1/2 C. water

3 egg whites
24 milk chocolate candy
    kisses, unwrapped
1 (7 oz.) jar marshmallow
    crème

Preheat oven to 350°. Line 24 2 1/2" muffin cups with paper liners. In a large bowl, beat together cake mix, 2 tablespoons graham cracker crumbs, water and egg whites at high speed for 2 minutes. Fill prepared muffin cups 2/3 full with batter. Top the batter in each muffin cup with 1 chocolate kiss, pressing down lightly. Spoon 1 teaspoon graham cracker crumbs onto each cupcake. Bake in oven for 18 to 25 minutes. Remove from oven and top each cupcake with 1 teaspoon marshmallow crème, dipping a spoon in hot water to prevent sticking. Return to oven for about 1 minute to melt marshmallow slightly.

Praline Chocolate Cake

Makes 14 servings

2 C. milk
2 1/2 C. sugar, divided
1 1/2 C. butter, softened, divided
8 (1 oz.) squares unsweetened chocolate, chopped
4 eggs, separated

2 1/3 C. cake flour
2 tsp. baking powder
1/2 C. chopped almonds, toasted*
1 C. chopped pecans, divided, toasted*
1/4 C. powdered sugar

Preheat oven to 325°. Grease a 10" tube pan and set aside. In a double boiler over medium heat, combine milk, 1 1/2 cups sugar, 1 cup butter and chopped chocolate. Bring to a boil, stirring occasionally. Remove from heat and let cool slightly. Stir in egg yolks, flour and baking powder. Transfer mixture to a medium mixing bowl and beat at medium speed for 2 minutes. In a separate bowl, beat egg whites until fluffy. Fold beaten egg whites into chocolate mixture and pour batter into prepared pan. Bake in oven for 50 minutes. Remove cake from oven and let cool in pan for 15 minutes before removing to a wire rack to cool. To make frosting, in a heavy saucepan over medium heat, heat remaining 1 cup sugar. When sugar is melted and slightly darkened, stir in toasted almonds and 1/2 cup toasted pecans. Mix well and spread mixture onto a greased baking sheet to cool. Once cooled, blend nut mixture in a blender or food processor until ground. In a medium bowl, cream remaining 1/2 cup butter until fluffy. Stir in ground nut mixture and powdered sugar, beating until smooth and creamy. Spread frosting over cooled cake. Garnish with remaining 1/2 cup toasted pecans.

* To toast, place chopped almonds and chopped pecans in a single layer on separate baking sheets. Bake at 350° for approximately 10 minutes or until nuts are golden brown.

Famous Chocolate Fanfare Tart

Makes 12 servings

1 3/4 C. flour, divided
2 T. brown sugar
4 1/2 C. chocolate chips,
 divided
6 T. cold butter, diced
2 to 3 T. milk
4 tsp. vanilla, divided

1/2 C. butter, melted and
 boiling
1 1/2 C. sugar
3 eggs
1 T. grated orange peel
1 C. heavy whipping cream

Preheat oven to 350°. To make crust, in a blender or food processor, combine 1 cup flour, brown sugar and 1 cup chocolate chips. Process until chocolate chips are finely ground. Add 6 tablespoons diced cold butter and process until mixture is crumbly. Add milk and 1 teaspoon vanilla and mix until dough is workable. Press dough into a greased 11" springform tart pan. Bake until crust is set. To make filling, in a medium bowl, combine 1 1/2 cups chocolate chips and 1/2 cup boiling butter. Stir until melted and smooth. In a separate bowl, combine sugar, eggs and remaining 3 teaspoons vanilla. Stir in melted chocolate and butter mixture. Add remaining 3/4 cup flour and grated orange peel. Mix well and pour mixture into baked tart crust. Bake for about 35 minutes, until tart is almost cooked throughout, being careful not to overbake. To make topping, in a medium saucepan over medium heat, bring heavy whipping cream to a boil. In a medium bowl, combine boiling heavy cream and remaining 2 cups chocolate chips and mix until smooth. Spread melted mixture over cooled tart. Refrigerate until ready to serve.

Cherry Chocolate Cobbler

Makes 18 servings

3 eggs, divided
1 pkg. 2-layer chocolate
   cake mix
3/4 C. butter, softened
4 C. powdered sugar, sifted
1 (8 oz.) pkg. cream cheese,
   softened

1 (21 oz.) can cherry
   pie filling
Heavy whipping cream
   for garnish

Preheat oven to 350°. Lightly grease and flour a 9x13" baking dish. In a large bowl, lightly beat 1 egg. Add chocolate cake mix and butter and beat until well blended. Press cake mixture into the bottom of prepared pan. In a medium bowl, combine sifted powdered sugar, cream cheese and remaining 2 eggs. Mix well and pour over cake mixture in pan. Spread cherry pie filling evenly over cream cheese layer. Bake for 30 to 40 minutes, until edges are lightly browned and center of cobbler is almost set. Let cool completely. Cover and chill in refrigerator until ready to serve. To serve, scoop cobbler into tea cups or bowls. Microwave until hot and garnish with 1 to 2 teaspoons heavy cream on top of each serving.

Life is like a box of chocolates... you never know what you're going to get.

Apricot Chocolate Torte

Makes 12 servings

1 lb. dried and coarsely
   chopped apricots
1/2 C. sugar
1 1/2 C. water
2 T. fresh lemon juice
1 3/4 C. plus 2 T. flour,
   divided
2 C. walnuts

1/2 C. chocolate chips
1/2 tsp. salt
1 tsp. vanilla
3/4 C. brown sugar
3/4 C. cold butter,
   cut into pieces
Chocolate curls for garnish

Preheat oven to 350°. To make filling, in a medium saucepan over low heat, combine apricots, sugar, water, lemon juice, and 2 tablespoons flour. Cook about 10 minutes, stirring frequently, until thickened and most of the liquid is absorbed. Remove from heat and let cool. To make dough, in a blender or food processor, combine walnuts and chocolate chips and pulse until mixture is coarsely chopped. In a large mixing bowl, beat together walnut mixture, remaining 1 3/4 cups flour, salt, vanilla and brown sugar. Using a pastry blender, cut in butter until mixture is crumbly. Place 2/3 of the dough in the bottom and 1 1/2" up sides of a greased 9 1/2" springform pan. Spread apricot filling evenly over crust and crumble remaining 1/3 of the dough over filling. Bake for 50 to 60 minutes, until golden brown. Remove to a wire rack and let torte cool completely in pan before removing sides of springform pan. If desired, garnish top of torte with chocolate curls. Torte may be made up to 1 day ahead, covered and chilled in refrigerator until ready to serve.

Chocolate Cappuccino Cheesecake

Makes 12 servings

1 C. crushed chocolate
    wafer cookies
1/4 C. butter, softened
1 C. plus 2 T. sugar, divided
1/4 tsp. cinnamon
3 (8 oz.) pkgs. cream cheese,
    softened
3 eggs
8 (1 oz.) squares semi-sweet
    chocolate
1 C. plus 2 T. heavy
    whipping cream,
    divided

1 C. sour cream
1/4 tsp. salt
2 tsp. instant coffee granules
1/4 C. hot water
1/4 C. plus 2 T. Kahlua,
    divided
2 tsp. vanilla
2 T. powdered sugar

Preheat oven to 350°. Grease a 9" or 10" springform pan. In a medium bowl, combine crushed chocolate wafer cookies, butter, 2 tablespoons sugar and cinnamon. Mix well and press mixture into the bottom of prepared pan and set aside. In a medium mixing bowl, beat cream cheese at medium speed until smooth. Gradually add remaining 1 cup sugar and mix until well blended. Add eggs, one at a time, mixing well after each addition. Beat mixture at low speed until smooth and set aside. In a double boiler over medium heat, combine semi-sweet chocolate squares and 2 tablespoons heavy whipping cream. Heat mixture, stirring occasionally, until melted and smooth. Add melted chocolate mixture to cream cheese mixture

(Continued on next page)

and mix well. Stir in sour cream and salt. In a small bowl, combine instant coffee granules and 1/4 cup hot water, stirring until coffee is completely dissolved. Add coffee mixture, 1/4 cup Kahlua and vanilla to cream cheese mixture, beating until smooth. Pour over crust in prepared pan. Bake in oven for 45 minutes or until center of cheesecake is just firm. Turn off oven and leave cheesecake in oven with the door open for 45 minutes. Remove cheesecake from oven and chill in refrigerator. To make flavored whipped topping, in a medium mixing bowl, beat remaining 1 cup heavy whipping cream until soft peaks form. Add powdered sugar and remaining 2 tablespoons Kahlua, mixing until smooth. Serve cooled cheesecake with dollops of flavored whipped topping.

Never mind about 1066 William the Conqueror or 1087 William II. Such things are not going to affect one's life...but 1932 Mars Bar, 1936 Maltesers and 1937 the Kit Kat...these date are milestones in history and should be seared into the memory of every child in the country. ~ Roald Dahl

White Chocolate Cheesecake with Chocolate Brandy Sauce

Makes 12 servings

3 (8 oz.) pkgs. cream cheese, softened
3/4 C. sugar
1/4 C. flour
3 eggs
4 (1 oz.) squares white chocolate

1/2 tsp. vanilla
1 1/2 C. heavy whipping cream, divided
2 C. finely chopped white chocolate
2 oz. brandy

Preheat oven to 300°. Wrap the outside of a 10" springform pan with aluminum foil and grease the inside of the pan. In a large mixing bowl, beat cream cheese, sugar and flour at medium speed until lightened and fluffy. Add eggs, one at a time, beating well after each addition. In a double boiler over medium heat, place white chocolate squares. Heat, stirring occasionally, until melted. Add melted white chocolate to cream cheese mixture and beat at low speed until blended. Slowly add vanilla and 1/2 cup heavy whipping cream. Mix until well blended and pour into prepared springform pan. Fill a large saucepan or shallow bowl with warm water. Place springform pan in water bath and bake in oven for 50 to 60 minutes or until center of cheesecake is just firm. Let cheesecake cool at room temperature for 1 hour. Refrigerate until set before removing from pan. To make Chocolate Brandy Sauce, in a medium saucepan over medium heat, bring remaining 1 cup heavy cream to a boil, being careful to not let cream boil over. Place chopped white chocolate in a medium bowl. Pour hot cream over white chocolate and stir with a wooden spoon until chocolate is melted. Add brandy and stir until well mixed. Before serving, drizzle sauce over cooled cheesecake.

Chocolate Mint Cheesecake

Makes 12 servings

1 (9 oz.) pkg. thin chocolate
   wafers
21 (1 oz.) squares bittersweet
   chocolate, divided
2 C. plus 3 T. sugar, divided
8 T. butter, divided
4 (8 oz.) pkgs. cream cheese,
   softened

4 eggs
1 C. heavy whipping cream,
   divided
1/2 C. cocoa powder
1 T. vanilla
1 tsp. peppermint extract
1 1/2 C. sour cream

Preheat oven to 350°. Grease a 9″ springform pan. In a blender combine thin chocolate wafers and 3 bittersweet chocolate squares. Blend until crumbly. Transfer mixture to a medium bowl and add 3 tablespoons sugar. In a glass measuring cup, place 7 tablespoons butter. Heat in microwave until melted. Mix melted butter into ground mixture. Press mixture into the bottom of prepared springform pan and set aside. In a double boiler over medium heat, place 12 bittersweet chocolate squares. Heat, stirring occasionally, until melted. Remove from heat and let cool slightly. Add cream cheese, 1 3/4 cups sugar, 1/2 cup heavy whipping cream, cocoa powder, vanilla and peppermint extract. Mix well and pour mixture over crust in prepared pan. Bake in oven for 1 hour. Remove from oven and chill in refrigerator overnight. Preheat oven to 350°. In a small bowl, combine sour cream and remaining 1/4 cup sugar, mixing until smooth. Pour mixture over cooled cheesecake and bake in oven for 20 minutes. Chill in refrigerator for an additional 6 to 8 hours. To make icing, in a small saucepan over medium heat, combine remaining 1/2 cup heavy cream and remaining 1 tablespoon butter. Mix well and add remaining 6 bittersweet chocolate squares, stirring until melted. Remove from heat and let cool slightly. Drizzle icing over cooled cheesecake or, using a pastry bag, pipe icing in a lattice pattern over cheesecake.

Irish Cream Chocolate Cheesecake

Makes 12 servings

1 1/2 C. crushed chocolate
    wafer cookies
1/3 C. powdered sugar
1/3 C. plus 1/4 C. cocoa
    powder, divided
1/4 C. butter, melted
3 (8 oz.) pkgs. cream
    cheese, softened

1 1/4 C. sugar
3 T. flour
3 eggs
1/2 C. sour cream
1/4 C. Irish cream liqueur

Preheat oven to 350°. Grease a 9" springform pan. In a large bowl, combine crushed chocolate wafer cookies, powdered sugar and 1/3 cup cocoa powder. Add melted butter and mix well. Press mixture into the bottom of prepared springform pan. Bake in oven for 10 minutes, remove from oven and set aside. Increase oven temperature to 450°. In a large mixing bowl, beat together cream cheese, sugar, remaining 1/4 cup cocoa powder and flour at medium speed until well blended and smooth. Add eggs, one at a time, mixing well after each addition. Reduce speed to low and add sour cream and Irish cream liqueur, mixing until well blended. Pour mixture over crust in prepared pan. Bake in oven for 10 minutes. Reduce oven temperature to 250° and bake for 1 hour. Remove cheesecake from oven and chill in refrigerator until set. Before serving, remove sides of springform pan.

Candies

Chocolate Filled Bon-Bons

Makes 4 dozen

3/4 C. shortening
1/2 C. sugar
1/4 C. brown sugar
1 egg
2 tsp. vanilla
1/2 tsp. almond extract
1 3/4 C. flour

1/2 tsp. baking powder
1/2 tsp. salt
1/2 C. finely chopped
    walnuts
48 milk chocolate kisses,
    unwrapped
Chocolate frosting, optional

Preheat oven to 350°. In a medium mixing bowl, beat together shortening, sugar and brown sugar at medium speed until fluffy. Add egg, vanilla and almond extract and mix until well blended. Add flour, baking powder, salt and chopped walnuts and mix well. Form mixture into 1" balls. Press each ball around 1 chocolate kiss so that the kiss is completely covered. Set balls 1" apart on ungreased baking sheets. Bake in oven for 12 minutes. Remove from oven and let cool on a wire rack. If desired, frost bon-bons with chocolate frosting.

Forget love. I'd rather fall in chocolate!

Chewy Chocolate Candies

Makes 2 dozen

2 T. butter
2 (1 oz.) squares
   unsweetened chocolate
1/2 C. light corn syrup

3 C. powdered sugar, divided
3/4 C. powdered milk
1 tsp. vanilla

In a double boiler over medium heat, combine butter and unsweetened chocolate squares. Heat, stirring occasionally, until melted. Remove from heat and let cool slightly. In a medium mixing bowl, beat melted chocolate mixture, corn syrup and 2 cups powdered sugar at medium speed. Add powdered milk and vanilla and mix until well blended. The dough should be stiff. Sprinkle a flat surface with remaining 1 cup powdered sugar. Turn dough out onto surface and knead until powdered sugar is incorporated. Shape dough into 24 small logs. Wrap in waxed paper and chill in refrigerator until ready to serve.

Turtle Chocolates

Makes 2 dozen

1 (4 oz.) pkg. pecan halves
24 individual caramels,
   unwrapped

1 tsp. shortening
1 C. chocolate chips

Preheat oven to 300°. Cover baking sheets with aluminum foil and lightly grease the foil. Place groups of 3 pecan halves in a Y shape on the foil and place 1 caramel over the center of each Y, pressing down slightly. Bake in oven for 9 to 10 minutes, until caramel is just melted. In a double boiler over low heat, combine shortening and chocolate chips, stirring occasionally, until melted. Spoon a little of the melted chocolate mixture over each turtle, spreading until the caramel is completely covered. Chill turtles in refrigerator for 30 minutes, until set.

T'will make old women young and fresh,

create new motion of the flesh.

And cause them long for you know what,

if they but taste of chocolate.

Rocky Road Candies

Makes 2 dozen

1 (12 oz.) pkg. chocolate chips
2 T. butter
1 (14 oz.) can sweetened
    condensed milk

2 1/2 C. dry-roasted peanuts
1 (16 oz.) pkg. miniature
    marshmallows

Line a 9x13" baking dish with waxed paper. In a medium microwave-safe bowl, combine chocolate chips and butter. Microwave on high until melted, stirring after every 30 seconds. Remove from microwave and stir in sweetened condensed milk, dry-roasted peanuts and miniature marshmallows. Pour mixture into prepared pan. Chill in refrigerator until set. Before serving, cut into small squares.

Martha Washington Candies

Makes 8 dozen

1 C. butter or margarine,
   softened
4 C. powdered sugar
1 (14 oz.) can sweetened
   condensed milk

2 C. shredded coconut
2 C. chopped pecans
2 tsp. vanilla
2 C. chocolate chips

Line two baking sheets with waxed paper and set aside. In a large mixing bowl, combine butter, powdered sugar and sweetened condensed milk at low speed until blended. Using a wooden spoon, stir in shredded coconut, chopped pecans and vanilla. Mix well and chill mixture in refrigerator until firm enough to handle. Form mixture into 1" balls and place on prepared baking sheets. In a double boiler over medium low heat, melt chocolate chips. Insert a toothpick into each ball and dip in melted chocolate. Return dipped balls to baking sheets to cool.

And above all...think chocolate!
~ Betty Crocker

White Chocolate Bark Candy

Makes 1 pound

**1 (10 oz.) pkg. vanilla
   baking chips**

**2 tsp. vegetable oil
1 1/2 C. M&M's**

Line a baking sheet with waxed paper or aluminum foil. In a large glass measuring cup or bowl, combine vanilla chips and vegetable oil. Microwave on high, stirring after every 30 seconds, until vanilla chips are melted. Remove from microwave and stir until smooth. Let cool for 2 minutes. Add M&M's, mixing until fully incorporated. Spread mixture onto prepared pan. Chill in refrigerator for 10 minutes, until hardened. To serve, break bark candy into pieces.

Marshmallow Chocolate Candies

Makes 2 dozen

1/2 C. butter
1 (14 oz.) can sweetened
   condensed milk
1 (6 oz.) pkg. butterscotch chips
1 (12 oz.) pkg. chocolate chips

1 C. chopped pecans
1 (10 1/2) oz. pkg. miniature
   marshmallows
1 tsp. vanilla

   In a medium saucepan over medium heat, combine butter and sweetened condensed milk. Bring to a boil, stirring occasionally, and remove from heat. Stir in butterscotch chips and chocolate chips, stirring until chips are melted. Add chopped pecans, miniature marshmallows and vanilla and stir until fully incorporated. Drop mixture by tablespoonfuls onto waxed paper. Chill in refrigerator until set.

I owe it all to little chocolate donuts. ~ John Belushi

104

Layered Caramel Chocolates

Makes 8 dozen

2 C. milk chocolate chips, divided
1/2 C. butterscotch chips, divided
3/4 C. creamy peanut butter, divided
1/4 C. butter
1 C. sugar

1/4 C. evaporated milk
1 1/2 C. marshmallow crème
1 tsp. vanilla
1 1/2 C. chopped salted peanuts
1 (14 oz.) pkg. individual caramels, unwrapped
1/4 C. heavy whipping cream

Lightly grease a 9x13" baking dish and set aside. In a small saucepan over low heat, combine 1 cup milk chocolate chips, 1/4 cup butterscotch chips and 1/4 cup peanut butter. Cook, stirring constantly, until melted and smooth. Spread mixture over the bottom of prepared pan. Chill in refrigerator until set. In a medium heavy saucepan over medium high heat, place butter. Heat until butter is melted and add sugar and evaporated milk. Bring mixture to a boil, stirring constantly, for 5 minutes. Remove from heat and stir in marshmallow crème, 1/4 cup peanut butter and vanilla. Fold in chopped peanuts and spread mixture over cooled layer in pan. Return to refrigerator until set. In a separate saucepan over low heat, place caramels and heavy whipping cream. Heat, stirring occasionally, until melted and smooth. Spread caramel mixture over cooled layers in pan and return to refrigerator until set. In a separate saucepan over low heat, combine remaining 1 cup milk chocolate chips, remaining 1/4 cup butterscotch chips and remaining 1/4 cup peanut butter. Cook, stirring constantly, until melted and smooth. Spread over caramel layer and chill in refrigerator for at least 1 hour. Before serving, cut candies into 1" squares.

Easy Cracker Candy

Makes 10 to 12 servings

1 sleeve saltine crackers	**2 C. chocolate chips**
1 C. butter	**3/4 C. chopped walnuts**
3/4 C. sugar	

Preheat oven to 425°. Arrange saltine crackers in a single layer on a baking sheet. In a medium saucepan over medium heat, place butter. Heat, stirring occasionally, until butter is melted. Stir in sugar and bring to a low boil. Let boil for 3 minutes, stirring constantly, being careful not to burn. Drizzle hot sugar mixture over saltine crackers on baking sheet. Bake in oven for 5 minutes or until edges of crackers begin to brown. Remove from oven and immediately sprinkle chocolate chips over crackers, spreading chocolate chips with a spatula as they melt. Sprinkle with chopped walnuts and press walnuts gently in chocolate. Chill in refrigerator until hardened. To serve, break into pieces.

Coffee, Chocolate and Men...
Some things are just better
when they're rich!

Chow-Mein Chocolates

Makes 2 dozen

2 C. chocolate chips
2 C. butterscotch chips

2 1/2 C. dry-roasted peanuts
4 C. chow-mein noodles

Cover a baking sheet with waxed paper and set aside. In a double boiler over medium heat, combine chocolate chips and butterscotch chips. Heat, stirring occasionally, until chips are melted. Remove from heat and stir in peanuts and chow-mein noodles. Stir until fully coated. Drop mixture by tablespoonfuls onto prepared baking sheet. Chill in refrigerator until set.

Toffee Bits

Makes 3 dozen

2/3 lb. vanilla flavored
   confectioners coating
1 (10 oz.) pkg. vanilla
   baking chips

1 (12 oz.) can salted peanuts
1/2 (6 oz.) pkg. Heath Bits
   O' Brickle almond
   toffee bits

Cover baking sheets with waxed paper and set aside. In a double boiler over medium heat, place confectioners coating. Heat, stirring constantly, until melted and smooth. Add vanilla baking chips and stir until chips are melted. Stir in peanuts and almond toffee bits. Remove from heat and drop mixture by tablespoonfuls onto prepared baking sheets. Chill in refrigerator until set.

As with most fine things, chocolate has its season. There is a simple memory aid that you can use to determine whether it is the correct season to order chocolate: any month whose name contains the letter A, E or U is the proper time for chocolate.

Homemade Candy Bars

Makes 2 dozen

1/2 C. butter, softened
1 C. sugar
3 eggs
1 C. flour
1/4 C. cocoa powder
2/3 C. chopped almonds

2 C. shredded coconut
1 (14 oz.) can sweetened
   condensed milk
1 (16 oz.) container
   chocolate frosting

Preheat oven to 350°. Grease a 9x13" baking dish. In a medium bowl, cream together butter and sugar. Add eggs, one at a time, beating well after each addition. Stir in flour and cocoa powder, mixing until evenly incorporated. Press mixture evenly onto the bottom of prepared pan. Bake in oven for 15 to 20 minutes. Remove from oven and immediately sprinkle chopped almonds and shredded coconut over crust. Drizzle sweetened condensed milk over almonds and coconut. Return pan to oven for an additional 15 minutes or until bars are golden brown. Remove from oven and let cool completely before spreading with chocolate frosting. To serve, cut into squares.

Chocolate flows in deep, dark, sweet waves...a river to ignite my mind and alert my senses.

Red Hat Pretzel Buttons

Makes 2 dozen

24 circular pretzels　　　　　　**24 red M&M's**
24 milk chocolate kisses,
**　　unwrapped**

Preheat oven to 350°. Place pretzels in a single layer on a baking sheet. Place one chocolate kiss in the center of each pretzel. Bake in oven for 1 to 2 minutes, until kisses melt. Remove from oven and place one M&M in the center of each pretzel. Chill in refrigerator until set.

Mel Gibson on what women want:
After about 20 years of marriage, I'm finally starting to scratch the surface on that one. And I think the answer lies somewhere between conversation and chocolate.

Cookie Balls

Makes 3 dozen

1 lb. Oreo cookies, crushed
1 (8 oz.) pkg. cream cheese,
    softened

16 (1 oz.) squares white
    chocolate

In a large bowl, combine crushed Oreo cookies and cream cheese. Mix to form a stiff dough. Form mixture into 1" balls and place on prepared baking sheets. In a double boiler over medium low heat, melt white chocolate squares. Insert a toothpick into each ball and dip in melted chocolate. Return dipped balls to baking sheets to cool.

Peppermint Chocolate Wafers

Makes 3 dozen

6 (1 oz.) squares white chocolate, chopped
12 peppermint hard candies, crushed

1 C. chocolate chips
1 T. shortening

Line an 8" square baking dish with aluminum foil and set aside. In a large glass measuring cup or bowl, place chopped white chocolate. Microwave on high for 1 minute. Remove from oven and stir. Microwave for 10 to 20 second intervals, stirring until smooth. Remove from microwave and add crushed peppermint candies. Spread mixture in a thin layer into prepared pan. Chill in refrigerator for 10 minutes, until firm. Remove white chocolate mixture from dish and peel aluminum foil from chocolate. Break into pieces. Line baking sheets with waxed paper. In a small microwave-safe bowl, combine chocolate chips and shortening. Microwave on high for 1 minute. Remove from oven and stir. Microwave for 10 to 20 second intervals, stirring until smooth. Dip white chocolate pieces halfway into melted chocolate, shaking off excess. Place on prepared baking sheets. Chill in refrigerator until hardened and ready to serve.

Any sane person loves chocolate.

Cherry Fantasy Tarts

Makes 30 tarts

1 2/3 C. chocolate chips,
    divided
1/2 C. butter
3/4 C. sugar
2 eggs
1 tsp. vanilla

1/2 C. flour
30 maraschino cherries,
    stems removed
1 (14 oz.) can sweetened
    condensed milk

Preheat oven to 375°. Line miniature muffin pans with paper candy liners. In a medium microwave-safe bowl, combine 2/3 cup chocolate chips and butter. Microwave on high until chocolate is melted, stirring after every 20 to 30 seconds. Remove from microwave and stir until smooth. Let cool for 10 minutes. Stir in sugar, eggs and vanilla, mixing until well blended. Gradually stir in flour until smooth. Spoon mixture into prepared liners. Bake in oven for 12 to 14 minutes or until a toothpick inserted in center of tarts comes out clean. Remove from oven and immediately press one maraschino cherry into the center of each tart. Return to oven for an additional 2 minutes. Remove from oven and let cool for 5 minutes. In a small saucepan over medium low heat, combine sweetened condensed milk and remaining 1 cup chocolate chips. Heat, stirring constantly, for 2 to 3 minutes, until chocolate is melted and smooth. Spoon 1 teaspoon of the melted chocolate mixture over each tart. Chill tarts in refrigerator for at least 1 hour.

Research tells us that 14 out of any 10 individuals like chocolate.

Raspberry Truffles

Makes 2 dozen

22 (1 oz.) squares bittersweet chocolate, divided
6 T. butter

1/3 C. seedless raspberry jam
2 T. Chambord or raspberry liqueur

In a glass measuring cup, combine 10 bittersweet chocolate squares and butter. Microwave on high for 1 to 1 1/2 minutes, stirring after every 30 seconds, until melted and smooth. Remove from microwave and stir in raspberry jam and liqueur, mixing until well blended. Cover measuring cup with plastic wrap and chill in refrigerator until firm, up to 4 hours or overnight. Cover a baking sheet with waxed paper. Using a melon baller or small ice cream scoop, scrape mixture into balls and place on prepared baking sheet. Place in freezer for 1 hour. In a double boiler over medium heat, place remaining 12 bittersweet chocolate squares. Heat, stirring frequently, until melted and smooth. Spoon teaspoonfuls of melted chocolate over frozen chocolate balls on baking sheet. Chill in refrigerator until chocolate is set, about 30 minutes.

Sticks & Stones Candy Bark

Makes 18 servings

1 2/3 C. butterscotch chips, divided
1 1/2 C. milk chocolate chips
1/2 C. creamy peanut butter

2 C. pretzels sticks
2 C. dry-roasted peanuts
1 1/3 C. chocolate-covered raisins

Grease a 9x13" baking dish and set aside. In a large microwave-safe bowl, combine 1 1/3 cups butterscotch chips, milk chocolate chips and peanut butter. Microwave on high for 1 minute, stirring after 30 seconds. If necessary, microwave in 10 to 15 second intervals, stirring until chips are completely melted. Remove from microwave and fold in pretzels sticks, peanuts and chocolate-covered raisins, mixing until evenly coated. Spread mixture into prepared pan. Place remaining 1/3 cup butterscotch chips in a small, heavy-duty plastic bag. Microwave on high for 20 to 30 seconds. Knead plastic bag by hand until chips are melted. Cut a small corner from the bag and pipe melted butterscotch over candy bark in pan. Chill in refrigerator for 1 hour or until firm. To serve, break into bite-size pieces.

*What you see before you, my friend,
is the result of a lifetime of chocolate.*
~ Katherine Hepburn

Milk Chocolate Popcorn

Makes 12 to 14 servings

12 C. popped popcorn
1 (12 oz.) jar salted peanuts
1 3/4 C. milk chocolate chips

1 C. light corn syrup
1/4 C. butter or margarine

Preheat oven to 300°. Grease a large roasting pan and line baking sheets with waxed paper. Combine popcorn and peanuts in roasting pan. In a medium heavy saucepan over medium heat, combine milk chocolate chips, corn syrup and butter. Heat, stirring frequently, until mixture boils. Pour mixture over popcorn and peanuts in roasting pan, tossing until evenly coated. Bake in oven for 30 to 40 minutes, stirring after every 10 minutes. Remove from pan and let cool slightly in pan. Spread over prepared baking sheets and let cool completely. Store in an airtight container for up to 2 weeks.

A chocolate in the mouth is worth two on the plate.

Crispy Cocoa Bites

Makes 40 cocoa bites

6 T. butter or margarine
3 C. miniature marshmallows
1 2/3 C. peanut butter chips

1/3 C. cocoa powder
1/3 C. light corn syrup
5 C. crispy rice cereal

In a large saucepan over low heat, place butter. Heat, stirring occasionally, until melted. Add marshmallows, peanut butter chips and cocoa powder. Heat until peanut butter chips and marshmallows are melted, stirring constantly. Add corn syrup and crispy rice cereal and stir until evenly coated. Coat hands with butter and shape mixture into 1 1/2" balls. Place balls on baking sheets to cool.

Candy Bar Fudge

Makes 2 3/4 pounds

1/2 C. butter
1/3 C. cocoa powder
1/4 C. brown sugar
1/4 C. milk
3 1/2 C. powdered sugar
1 tsp. vanilla

30 individual caramels,
    unwrapped
1 T. water
2 C. salted peanuts
1/2 C. chocolate chips
1/2 C. milk chocolate chips

Grease an 8" square baking dish and set aside. In a microwave-safe bowl, combine butter, cocoa powder, brown sugar and milk. Microwave on high until mixture starts to boil. Remove from microwave and stir in powdered sugar and vanilla. Pour mixture into prepared pan. In a separate microwave-safe bowl, combine caramels and water. Microwave on high until caramels are melted, stirring after every 30 seconds. Stir in peanuts and spread mixture over chocolate layer in pan. In a small microwave-safe bowl, combine chocolate chips and milk chocolate chips. Microwave on high until melted, stirring until smooth. Spread over caramel layer in pan. Chill in refrigerator for 2 hours, until firm. To serve, cut into squares.

Giving chocolate to others is an intimate form of communication, a sharing of deep, dark secrets.

Candy Cane Fudge

Makes 2 1/4 pounds

2 (10 oz.) pkgs. vanilla
   baking chips
1 (14 oz.) can sweetened
   condensed milk

1/2 tsp. peppermint extract
1 1/2 C. crushed candy canes
Red or green food coloring

Line an 8" square baking dish with aluminum foil. Lightly grease the foil and set aside. In a medium saucepan over medium heat, combine vanilla baking chips and sweetened condensed milk. Heat, stirring frequently, until chips are almost melted. Remove from heat and continue stirring until completely melted. Stir in peppermint extract, crushed candy canes and drops of either red or green food coloring. Spread mixture evenly into prepared pan. Chill in refrigerator for 2 hours. To serve, cut into squares.

119

Peanut Butter Fudge

Makes about 50 pieces

1 1/2 C. sugar
2/3 C. evaporated milk
2 T. butter or margarine
1/4 tsp. salt
2 C. miniature marshmallows
1 1/2 C. chocolate chips

1 C. crunchy or creamy
    peanut butter
1 tsp. vanilla
1/2 C. chopped peanuts,
    optional

Line an 8" square baking dish with aluminum foil and set aside. In a medium heavy saucepan over medium heat, combine sugar, evaporated milk, butter and salt. Heat mixture, stirring constantly, and bring to a rolling boil. Boil, stirring constantly, for 4 to 5 minutes. Remove from heat and stir in marshmallows, chocolate chips, peanut butter and vanilla. Stir vigorously for 1 minute or until marshmallows are melted. Pour mixture into prepared pan and let cool for 1 minute. If desired, top with chopped peanuts, pressing down on peanuts slightly. Chill in refrigerator for 2 hours or until firm. Lift fudge from pan and remove foil. Cut fudge into pieces.

Once in a while I say, "Go for it"...and then I eat chocolate. ~ Claudia Schiffer

Index

121

COOKIES

CAKES

CANDIES

I never met a chocolate
I didn't like.